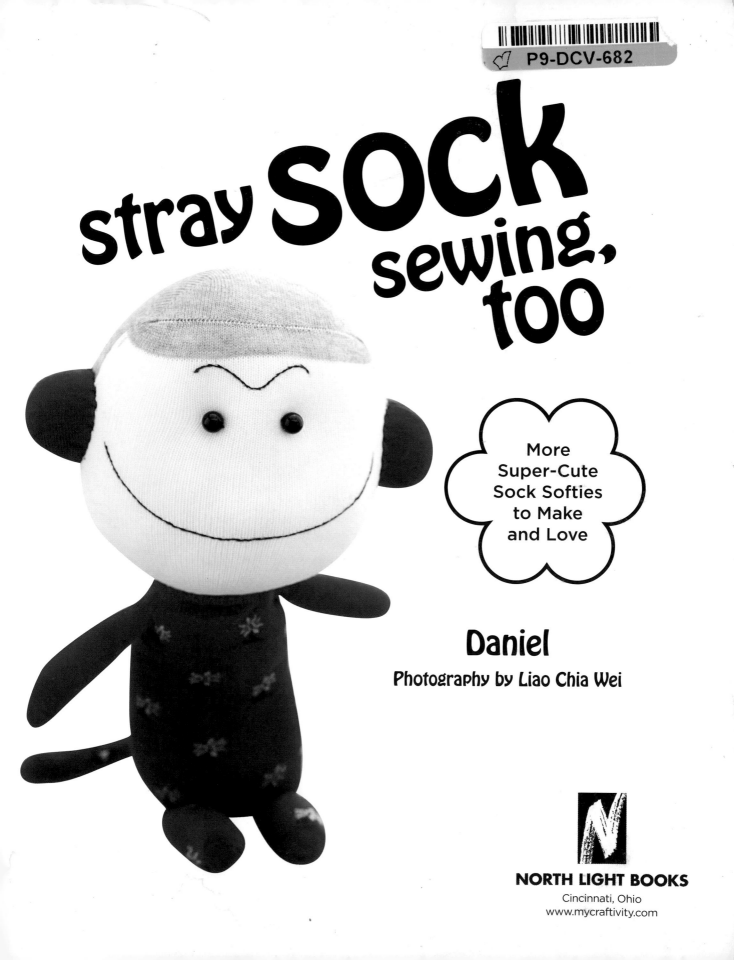

stray SOCK sewing, too

More Super-Cute Sock Softies to Make and Love

Daniel

Photography by Liao Chia Wei

NORTH LIGHT BOOKS
Cincinnati, Ohio
www.mycraftivity.com

English language rights, translation, & production by World Book Media LLC.
E-mail info@worldbookmedia.com
For international rights inquires contact: info@worldbookmedia.com
First Published in the United States of America by North Lights Books, an imprint of F+W Media, Inc., 4700 East Galbraith Road, Cincinnati, Ohio 45236. (800) 289-0963. First edition.

13 12 11 10 09   5 4 3 2 1

Distributed in Canada by Fraser Direct
100 Armstrong Avenue
Georgetown, ON, Canada L7G 5S4
Tel: (905) 877-4411

Distributed in the U.K. and Europe by David & Charles
Brunel House, Newton Abbot, Devon, TQ12 4PU, England
Tel: (+44) 1626 323200, Fax: (+44) 1626 323319
Email: postmaster@davidandcharles.co.uk

Distributed in Australia by Capricorn Link
P.O. Box 704, S. Windsor, NSW 2756 Australia
Tel: (02) 4577-3555

Library of Congress Cataloging-in-Publication Data
ISBN-13: 978-1-60061-907-6

media
www.fwmedia.com

Cover designer: Geoff Raker

Contents

Introduction

Always keep your sock dolls near, they help you find the sunshine in every situation.

When I make sock dolls, the daily pressures seem to fade away. I believe that they can reflect your mood and channel the innocence and fun hidden deep inside, no matter how old you are.

Four years ago, I made my first sock doll out of one of my stray socks. To my surprise, it captured my heart and I could not put it down. Since then, I have never questioned my sock doll-making journey. Each time I pick up a sock, whether it is brand new or old with holes, I try to see what little creature lies within. I prefer simple designs with little decoration, and I often try to maintain the lines of the sock so that people can easily tell what each doll is made from.

To share the enjoyment of this happy craft, I began teaching classes to people of all ages. When I see their expression after finishing their first sock doll, I am reminded that it is easy to find happiness in life. Happiness lies in the simple things we do and the enjoyment we find in everyday experiences.

Daniel

Part 1
Sock Doll Stories

We all have different stories and we may not look like we come from the same place, but inside all of us is the same ingredient, 100% love. As mischievous and easily distracted as we sock dolls may be, I think you'll find that we are perhaps the most perfect companions for any adventure. We weigh almost nothing, we eat very little, and we are super cool and fun to be with. So grab a needle and thread and sew up a new best friend!

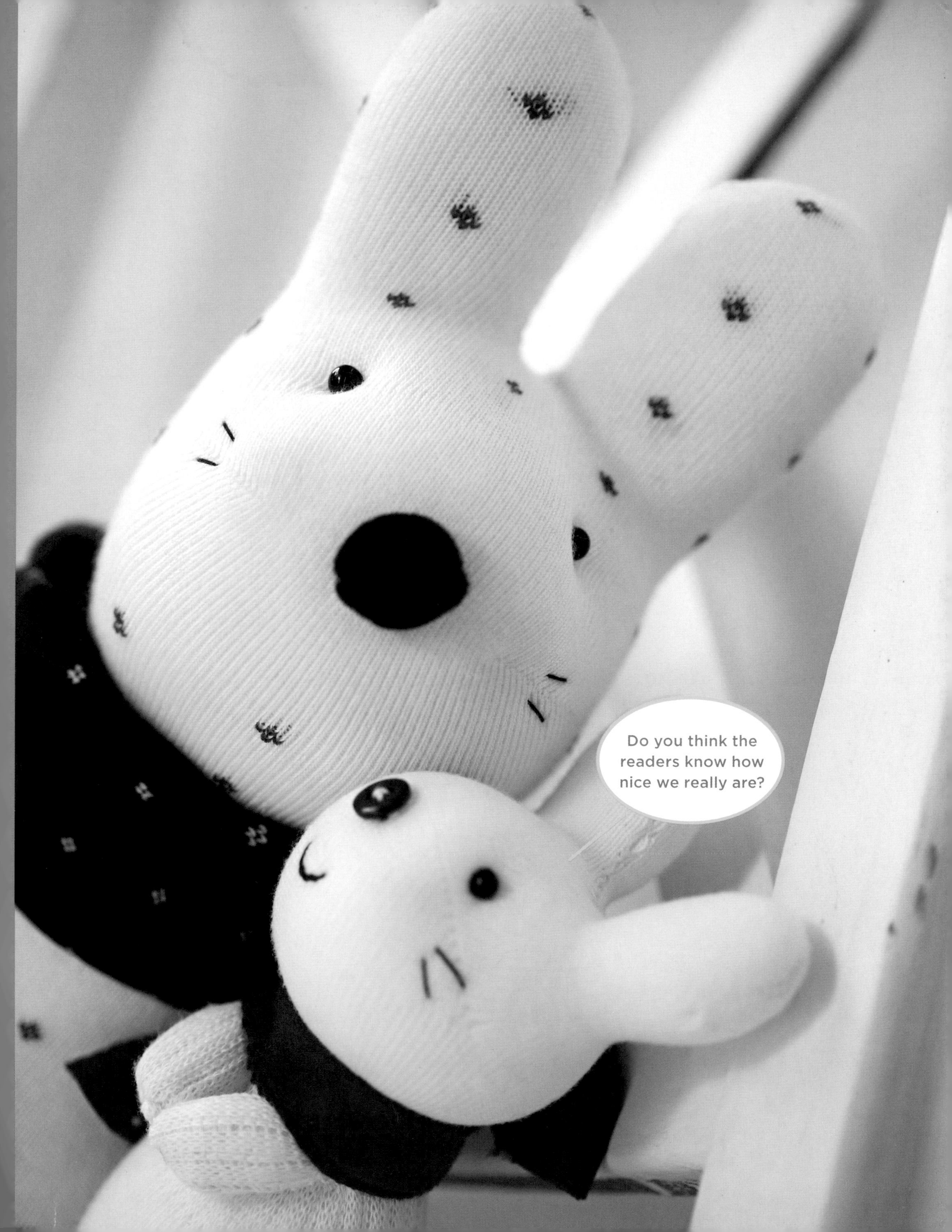
Do you think the
readers know how
nice we really are?

Grampa Penguin

[Chillin' Out]

A wise penguin knows that no matter where you are, you gotta be cool, even if it takes a little help from a fan. "When I go on vacation, I always take a fan. This planet is so darn hot!"

The Very Hungry Crocodile

[Follow Your Nose]

Although it's hard being away from home and not having your favorite food, sometimes you discover great things, like crab cakes and crackers! So remember "Try it, you might like it!"

Tree
Hugger

[Keepin' the Planet Clean]

"Why is it that some think it's ok to litter!? We've got this super cool planet and a lot of folks out there are just trashin' it. Just put the goods in the bin and we'll all have a nicer place to live."

What are people thinking?!

Chess
Mess

[Cats and Chess Just Don't Mix]

Have you ever tried to play chess with a cat?
It just doesn't work! There will be moments when
she looks like she is concentrating and planning
her next move, but don't fall for it! The minute
she thinks she is going to lose, she jumps on the
board, balances on the pieces trying to look
cute, and all just so she does not have to lose.
Trust me—they're cheaters!

Missing Pig

[Time Away]

Did you ever wonder what sock dolls do when you leave? They miss you! They stand in the window, waiting for your return, and feeling as if their world is coming to an end. Always be sure to give them lots of love when you come home so they know how much you missed them, too.

The Peeking Squirrel

[Remember, it's only a game.]

Sock dolls can be competitive when it comes to winning games, so there may be times when they need a gentle reminder about playing by the rules.

Sock dolls love a good game of hide and seek, as long as everyone plays fair. The seekers are not allowed to peek until they have counted to ten, but sometimes they just can't help themselves. It never hurts to review the rules before starting the game . . . just in case they have "forgotten".

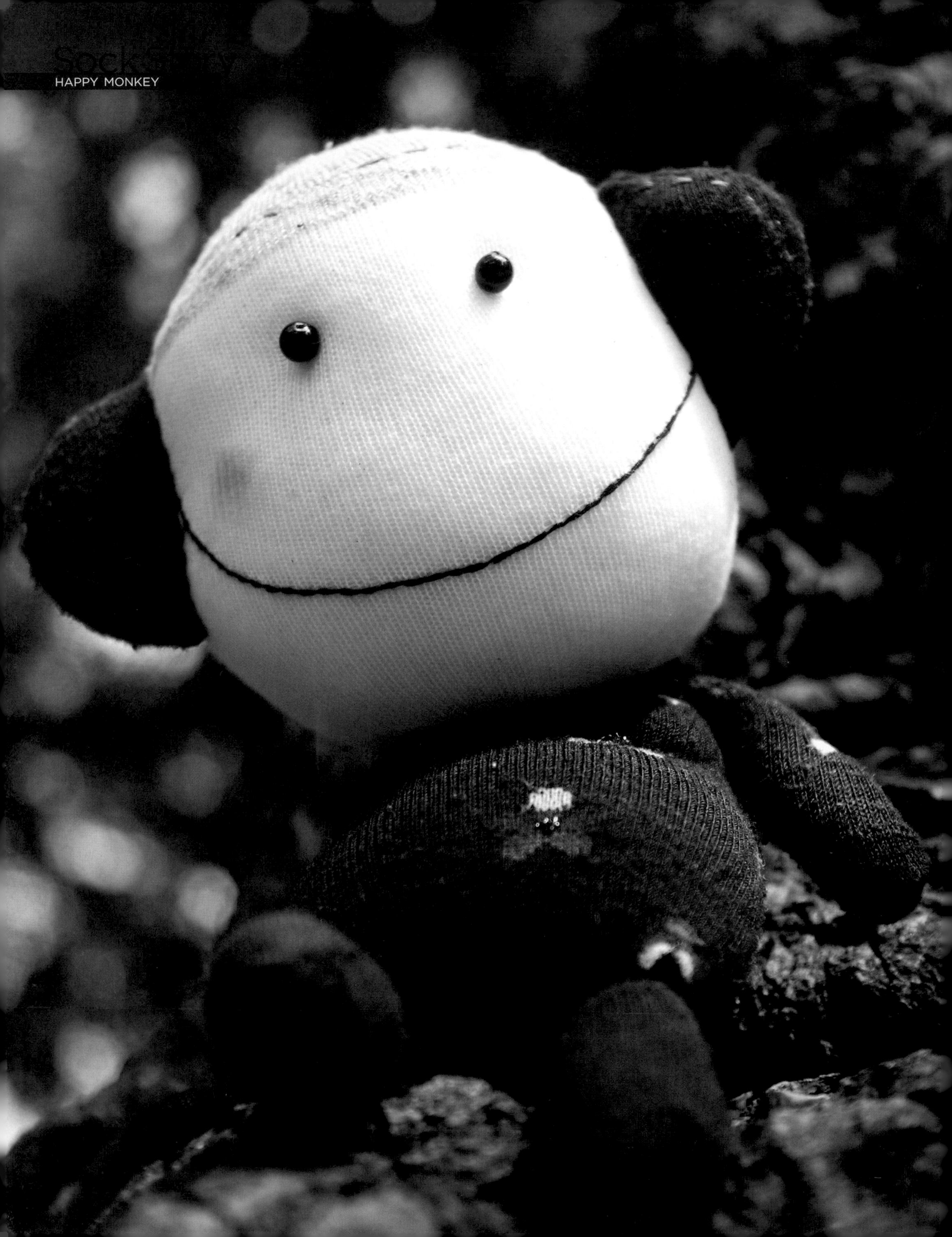

Happy Monkey

[Don't Worry, Be Happy!]

The secret to happiness lies within. The monkey does not compare his life to others or analyze the world. The sky is blue, the sun is shining, and with a big tree overhead, there is plenty of shade. Simple pleasures are all we need!

Best Friends

[Come Out and Play!]

Sock dolls are social creatures that LOVE
to be outside, except when it's raining!
To keep a smile stitched on their faces, set
up lots of play dates with their best friends.

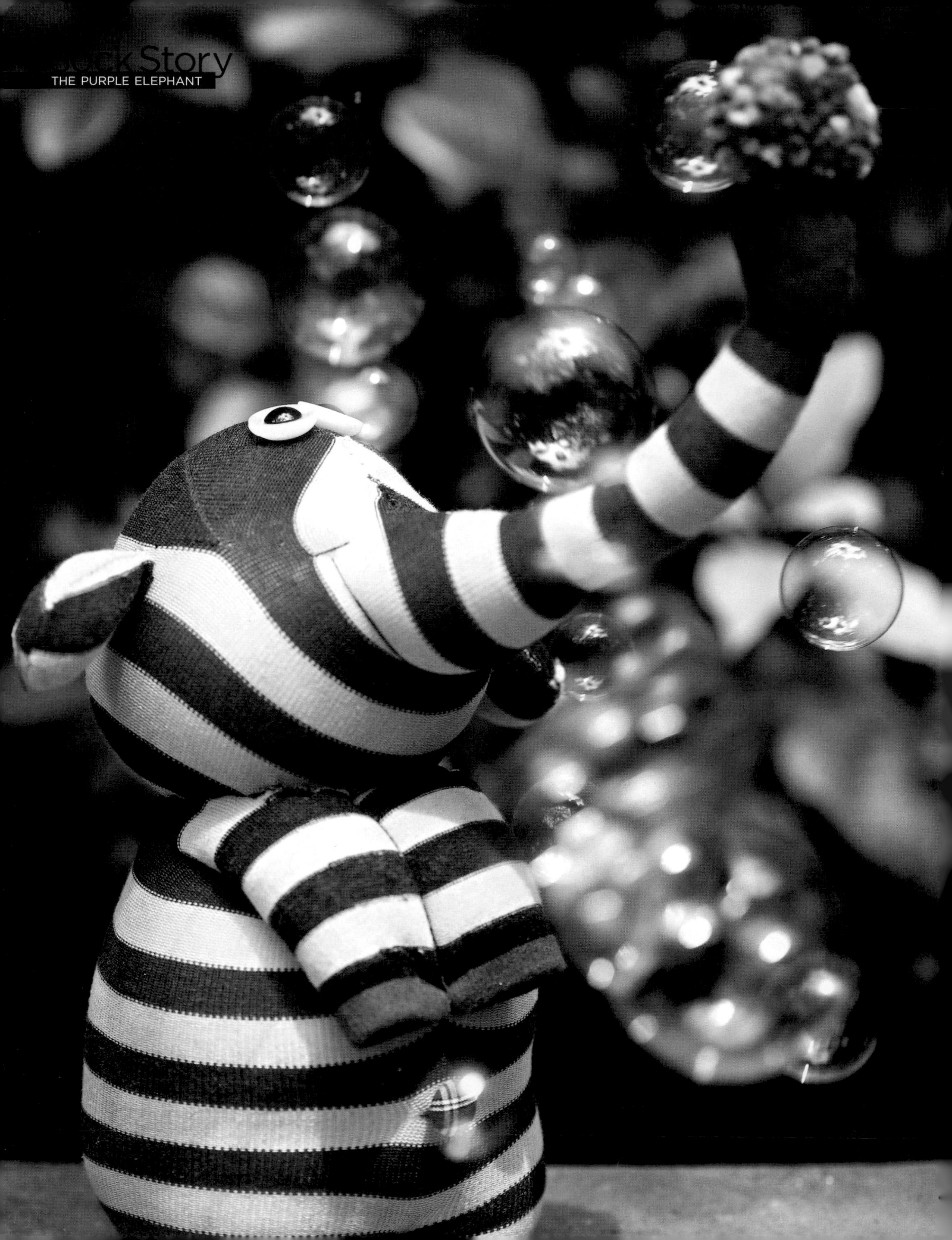

The Striped Elephant

[Elephants Never Forget to Have a Good Time]

Who can resist a fun-loving elephant? These zany creatures just can't help but keep you smiling, and the purple ones, forget about it! You'll laugh so hard you may just blow bubbles out your trunk.

Zen Tiger

[Year of the Tiger]

One of the twelve animals in the Chinese zodiac, the tiger is known to be unpredictable, rebellious, and impulsive. They are also among the most affectionate and generous. These clever cats can be a bit of a wild card in the sock doll kingdom, but don't underestimate how cuddly they can be.

Mrs. Honey

[Flower Power]

There is nothing sweeter than this little lady—one might even think that her belly was filled with honey. If you're having a bad day, take some time to smell the flowers with the sweetest sock doll of them all.

> The leapfrog races will begin in ten minutes.

Big Frog Little Frog

[Summer Camp]

Every sock doll loves summer camp. It teaches them self-confidence, independence, leadership, and most importantly, how to make friends!

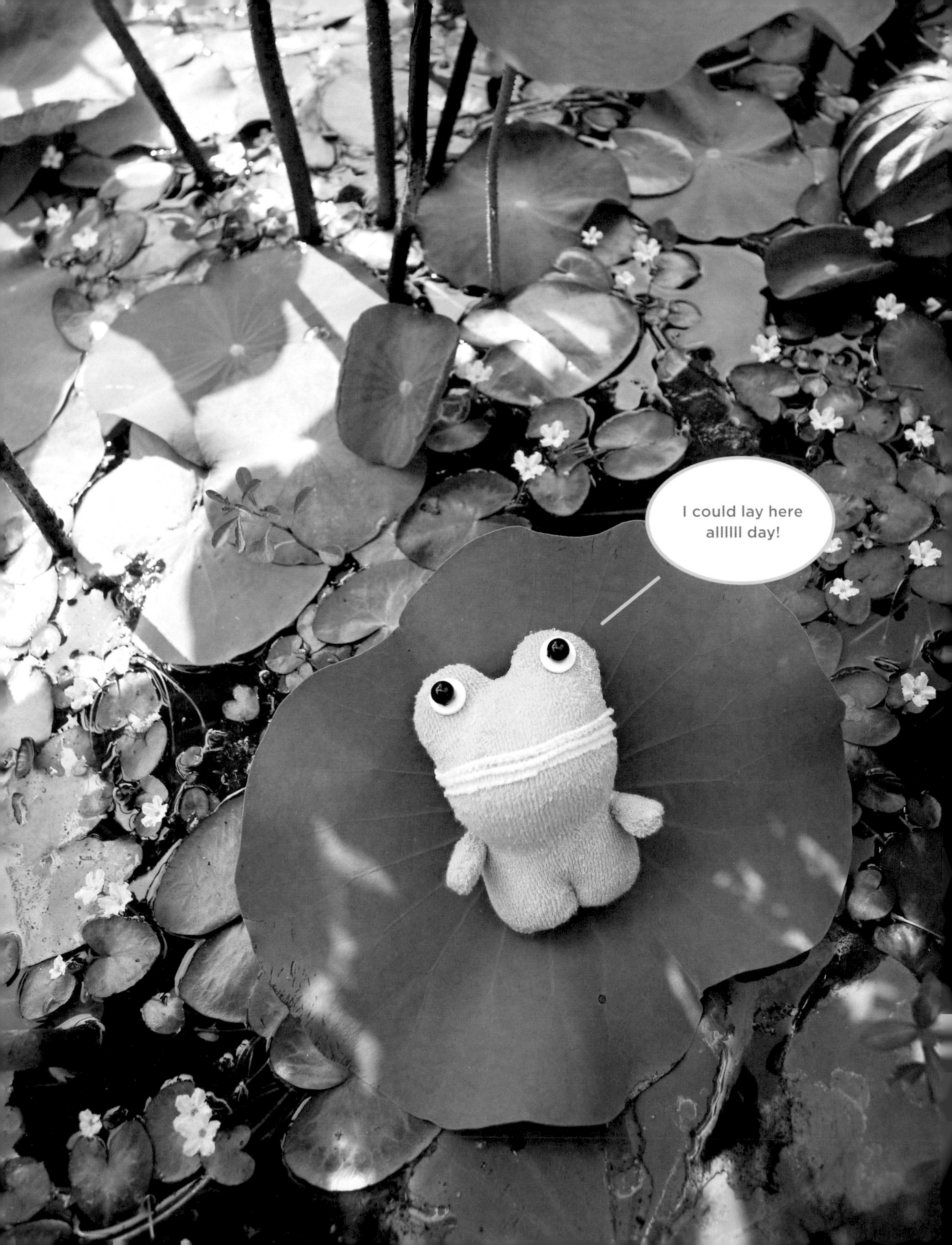
I could lay here alllll day!

"I love camp because I have lots of friends, there are new things to do every day, and places to cool off when the sun gets too hot."

Dinosock

[Seeing Eye-to-Eye]

When you come from different places you may not always agree on things. But remember, we're all made from socks and we all have stuffing on the inside, so how different can we really be?

Dragon and the Mouse

[Practicing Good Judgment]

Sock dolls are not known for remembering to play safely. One minute they can be sitting quietly and without a moment's notice, they are off doing something terribly unsafe! When playing, always supervise your sock dolls to ensure that no one needs to get stitched up because of a lapse in judgment.

Sad Monkey

[A Note on Sulking]

Warning. Sock dolls can be prone to sulking. Never let your socks act stinky, they must verbalize what is troubling them so you can find a solution together. Remember, a little tough love will help your over-sensitive sock doll learn how to find his smile.

Momma Bunny & Baby Bunny

[Moms Are the Best!]

"There's no one as great as my Mom. She always makes sure I'm wearing my scarf so I don't catch a cold, she takes me with her when she goes out, and she tucks me in at night leaving a bunny kiss on my forehead so I have sweet dreams!"

Miss Mini

[Happy-Go-Lucky]

Why is Miss Mini such a
happy girl? Because her
glass is half full!

This little pearl travels the world
and looks for the beauty in all things.

Cheshire Cat

[An Idle Mind Is a Dangerous Thing]

These little guys can be terribly mischievous when left to their own devices. To avoid things like spilled milk or missing socks, keep them entertained . . . at all times!

The Wise Owl

[Got Problems?]

The wise owl has answers. He is the all-seeing and the all-knowing. Look at those eyes, this guy doesn't miss a thing. He's the real deal!

Traveling Buddies

[The Bear Necessities?]

Always bring the "bear" necessities when going on a trip. In some cases this may mean a toothbrush, a bathing suit, and a good book. Other times it may mean your best friend. It is critical to have the right travel companion, so choose wisely!

Penny Penguin & Frankie Fish

[See the World from
a Different Perspective]

Sometimes you may feel like a fish
out of water when you go to new
places. But with the right friends,
you will always feel right at home.

Part 2
Sock Doll Sewing Projects

When you give your handmade sock doll to the people you love, you give them a loyal friend who will always be there for them. Every sock doll contains an important part of you because you have sewn each stitch with love.

Stitches You Need to Know

1 Slip Stitch This is an excellent hemming and finishing stitch because the thread is hidden inside a fold when it's sewn properly. The needle "tunnels" between the layers of the folded edges—hence the word "slip."

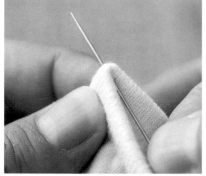  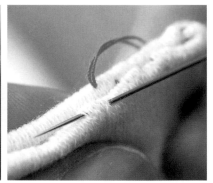

1 First, start the needle from behind the fold on the hem allowance, to hide the knot.

2 Take up around ⅛ inch (0.3 cm) of fabric; pull the thread. Then about 1/16 inch (1 mm) below the fold and slightly behind it, tunnel the needle for about ¼ inch (0.6 cm), before you bring it through for the next stitch.

3 Pull the thread, finish the one-stitch cycle, and repeat. You will see the thread is mostly hidden inside the material.

2 French Knot The French knot is a perfect stitch for small details such as eyes, whiskers, and other surface textures. They can be clustered in groups or added to the doll one by one.

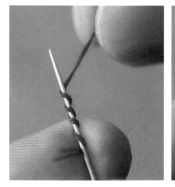 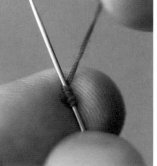  

1 Use your left hand to hold the needle and the thread. Tightly loop the thread around the needle two to three times with your right hand.

2 Compress the loops together, then hold the loops with your left hand.

3 Pull the needle out from the top, while holding onto the loops.

4 Tighten the knot.

3 Backstitch

Backstitch is great for outlining the shape of your dolls' hands, feet, and ears. Turn the fabric inside out; this will hide the stitches when you turn it right side out again to stuff.

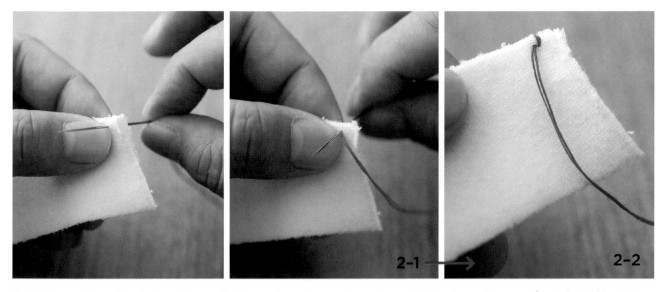

1 Right at the edge, bring the thread up from behind.

2 Loop the edge and go through the thread one more time, to make a knot. You'll want to make the stitches tight because once the doll is stuffed, the gaps can be expanded to expose the stuffing if you do not stitch tightly.

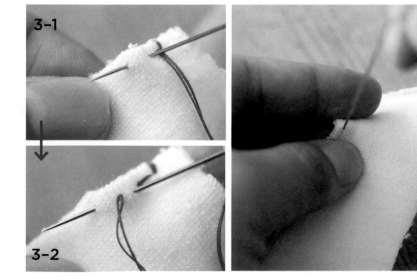

3 Run the needle through the material, around ⅛ inch (0.3 cm) in length. Re-enter the needle at the spot before where the previous stitch comes out. You've basically stitched back.

4 Use your thumb and index finger to hold the material flat, then pull the thread. To prevent the material from puckering together, do not pull the thread too taut.

5 This is how a completed backstitch should look.

4 **Ladder Stitch** Ladder stitching is a good way to attach dolls' parts together, and it's easy for beginners to do. You will want to make the stitches as small as possible to prevent the stuffing from leaking out.

 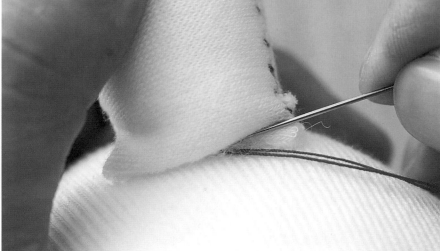

1 Place the parts in the right position, then sew from the main body part to the limb.

2 Before you push the thread through the limb, use the side of the needle to push the edges back while you stitch. You'll want to push the edge back while you make each stitch. This way, you can hide the stitches mostly inside the seam.

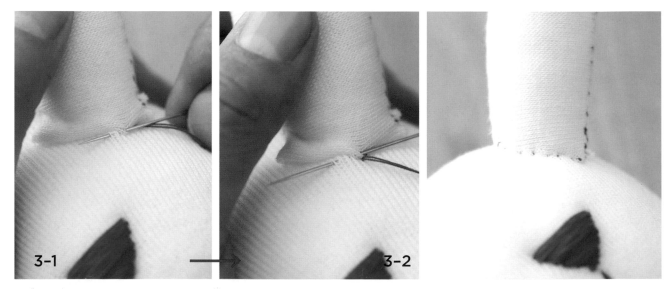

3-1 3-2

3 Stitch up and down through the two parts. Pin or hold the limbs together very steadily to avoid slipping.

4 This is how a finished section of ladder stitching should look.

5 Straight Stitch to Close off Gaps

The straight stitch is one of the easiest methods for sewing on large areas. You can use this stitch mainly to close the doll after you finished stuffing the body.

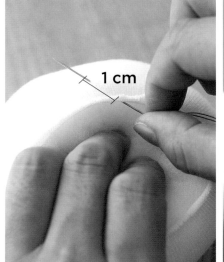

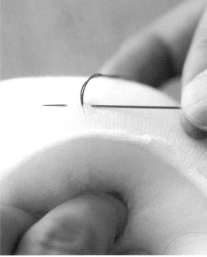

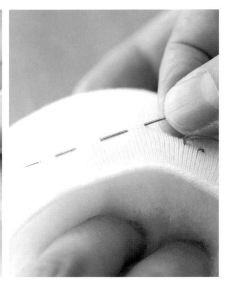

1 Bring the needle from inside to outside. Make the stitch no shorter than ³⁄₈ inch (1 cm). If the stitch is too short, it could become loose easily.

2 Use the backstitch to sew at the same location again to make sure the hold of the initial stitches is steady.

3 Use the straight stitch to go around in a circle. While you are sewing, push the stuffing inside.

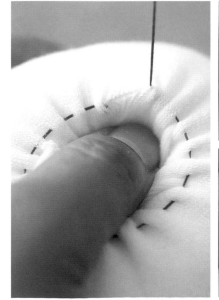

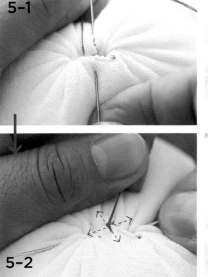

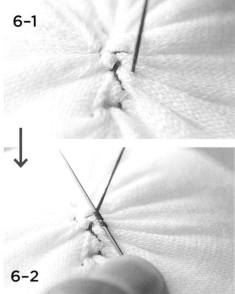

4 Pull the thread taut with each stitch while pressing the stuffing inside.

5 When you stitch the opening shut, you can make the final stitches in the shape of a cross. The cross stitches will make the close-off even tighter.

6 Get the needle out from the middle of the hole and make a French knot.

6 Split Running Stitch

The split running stitch can be used to outline a doll's mouth and eyes. You'll want to sew densely so that each stitch is blended together.

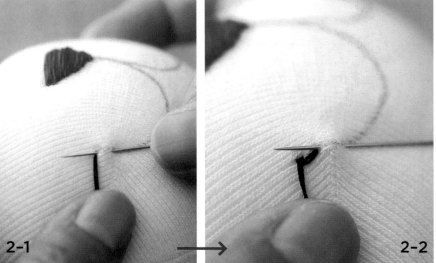

2-1 → 2-2

1 Use a colored pencil OR an erasable marking pen to trace the pattern first. Start the stitch from the inside, where you can hide the knot. Sew from the inside to outside.

2 Bring the needle ⅛ inch (0.3 cm) apart from the last stitch, then bring the needle from the front and back toward the last stitch. As the split stitch name implies, each new stitch is made through the previous one.

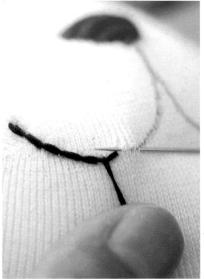

3 Trace the pattern with repeated stitches. Keep your stitch lengths as uniform as possible. When stitching a ∪ shape, pull the thread below the arc, then slip the needle between the threads for the next stitch.

4 When you've finished the first arc, you can turn the doll in a direction that is easy to work with for the next arc. I cross the needle to the other end of the arc, and stitch from the end toward the center.

5 Repeat the method used in step 2. If there is a ∩ shape, pull the thread above the arc to sew through.

7 How to Sew Buttons and Beads   Buttons or beads are mostly used for the eyes and noses of the sock dolls. You can also use them as decorative pieces for the body.

A: Using Cross Stitch for Buttons

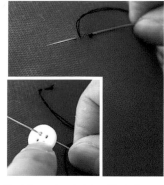 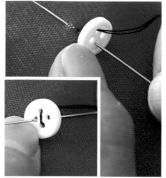 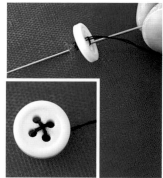

1   Use straight stitch to start. Pull the needle through one of the button holes.

2   Make stitches diagonally across the two holes, then repeat to stitch the other two holes across each other.

3   The stitches should appear like a cross.

B. Sewing a Button Shank

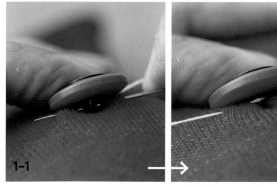

1   Using straight stitch, sew through the shank of the button. Repeat the stitch a few times, and make sure the shank is held down closely against the material. Make a knot to finish.

C. Sewing Beads

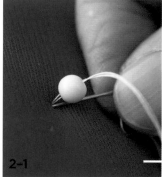 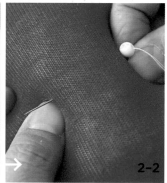

1   Sew the first bead at the desired location using straight stitch.

2   Bring the needle underneath the material, out at the location of the next bead.

3   Stitch through the second bead. After the last bead, make a French knot to finish.

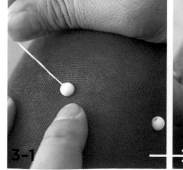 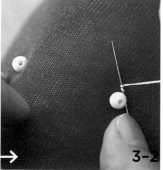

Step by Step

The Wise Owl

BASIC 1 Daniel's Classroom Tips

⊕ Finding a sock with the right texture is the key to making your owl lifelike. This little guy was made from a wool sock with a thick ribbed "featherlike" texture.

⊕ Keep leftover sock pieces for future use. Here you can see how the leftover part of a brown sock was used for the wings and beak.

✕ Materials and Tools

1 White thread for body
2 Black thread for eyes
3 Brown thread for wings and beak
4 Large scissors for cutting fabric
5 Tweezers/cuticle scissors for working with small socks, to help turn the fabric inside out, or to help when stuffing
6 Small, pointed scissors for seam ripping
7 Erasable marking pen
8 Two needles
9 Two black buttons with white circles for the eyes
10 One leg tube of a grey wool sock and a scrap of a brown sock
11 Stuffing (not shown in photo)

1 Using the erasable marking pen, outline the wings and beak pieces. The owl will be the size of a large fist, so be sure to scale the wings and beak for the body. The longest part of the wing should not exceed $1\,^{5}/_{8}$ inches (4 cm), and the length of the beak should not exceed $^{3}/_{4}$ of an inch (2 cm).

2 Turn the shapes inside out and use backstitches to sew the edges together.

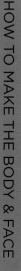

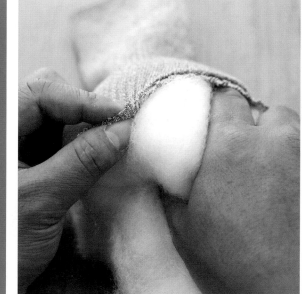

3 Turn the shapes right side out and fill the wings and beak with a small amount of stuffing. You may need to use the tweezers/cuticle scissors to fill in the small pockets.

4 Cut off the tube of the grey sock. Take some stuffing the size of your palm and mold it into a ball. Fill the tube and then use running stitches to sew the seam together.

5 Cut the extra sock near the cuff and sew the seam together with running stitches.

6 Before closing the seam, fit the beak into the small opening. Sew the beak into the opening and pull each stitch tight. Use ladder stitches to ensure the beak is securely attached and to seal off the opening.

7 Mold the body into a pear shape. The face should be smaller than the back of the body.

Whenever I have a question, I always ask an owl.

9 To make a raised eyebrow, pinch a portion of the sock and stuffing along the eyebrow marking. Sew through the sock and stuffing with backstitches to hold the eyebrow in place.

8 Mark two eyebrows approximately ³/₄ of an inch (2 cm) above the beak. Each eyebrow should be ¹/₄ inches (0.5 cm) wide.

10 Attach the eyes on the bottom, outside edge of each eyebrow. Make sure there is some distance between the eyebrow and each eye so the buttons lie flat.

11 Use ladder stitches to attach the wings. The top of the wings should line up with the center of the eyes.

Dinosock

BASIC 2 Daniel's Classroom Tips

● The key is to mold the neck evenly so that it forms a long, smooth, and straight shape.

● Try patterned or flowery socks to make different Dinosock characters.

✖ Materials and Tools

1 Black thread for eyes
2 White thread for body
3 Large scissors for cutting fabric
4 Tweezers/cuticle scissors for working with small socks, to help turn the fabric inside out, or to help when stuffing
5 Small, pointed scissors for seam ripping
6 Erasable marking pen
7 Two needles
8 Two larger white buttons and two smaller black buttons for eyes
9 One pair of flowered socks
10 Stuffing (not shown in photo)

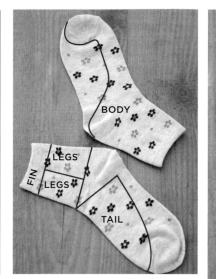

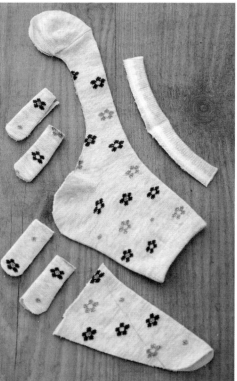

1 Outline the different body shapes as illustrated above.

2 Cut the shapes along the outlines. Cut the two square leg piece into four equal parts, one for each leg. Trim one end of each leg piece so that it has round edges. The cuff of the sock will become the fin.

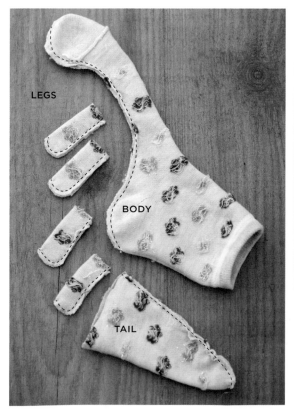

3 Use backstitches to sew the seams together as shown at left.

4 Fill each part with stuffing and form into the correct shapes. (See tips on the next page.)

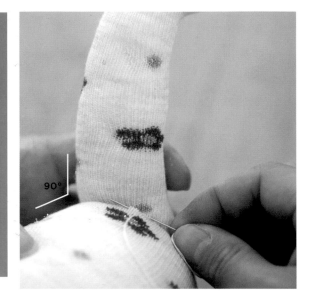

5 Holding the neck at a 90-degree angle to the body, use ladder stitches to attach the back of the neck to the body. Make sure the neck stands up straight so that you do not end up with a "depressed" Dinosock, whose head is bent toward the ground.

TIPS STUFFING YOUR DINOSOCK

⚙ **BODY** Begin by pushing a small ball of stuffing into the head. For the neck, you will need a handful of stuffing, about the size of a small fist. As you push the stuffing into the neck, add it evenly and with strong pressure so the neck is smooth and dense enough to stand up on its own.

⚙ **TAIL** Take a large handful of stuffing and push it into the tail. Mold the tail into a cone shape.

⚙ **LEGS** Use a small amount of stuffing to fill legs and shape each into an oval.

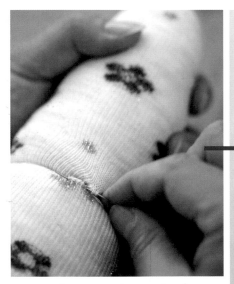

6 Ladder stitch the tail securely to the body.

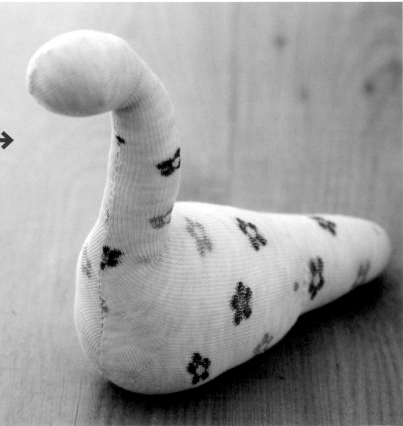

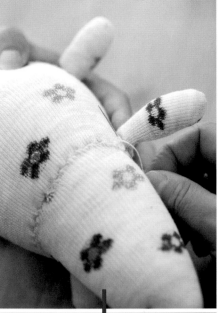

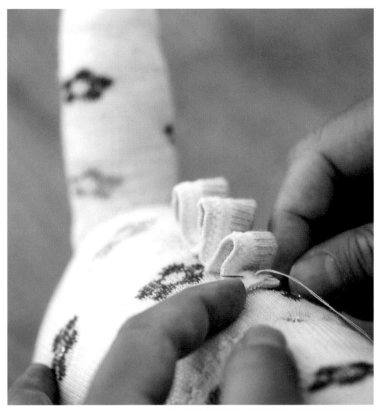

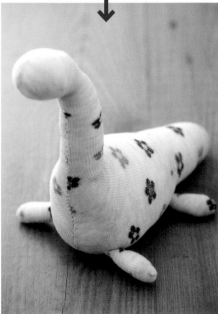

7 Mark the location of the legs on the body. Be sure they are symmetrically positioned on each side. Ladder stitch the legs onto the body.

8 Use a thin strip of the cuff to make the Dinosocks' fin. Fold the cuff to form small ripples. Stitch the wavy fin onto the Dinosock's back.

9 Position the smaller black button on top of the larger white button to make the pupil. Sew the buttons together and attach them to the head.

I love your new green outfit!

Big Frog

BASIC 3 Daniel's Classroom Tips

⊗ A cotton or wool sock will provide a firm and thicker textured frog. To achieve a more nostalgic feel, use an old washed out sock that carries with it some history.

⊗ To keep the big-mouthed frog company, use a baby sock to make a mini frog companion.

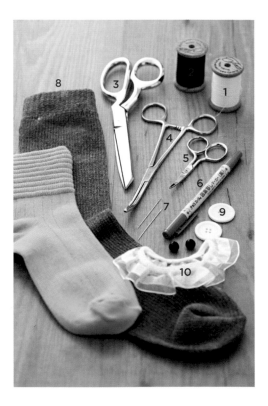

⊗ Materials and Tools

1 White thread for body

2 Black thread for eyes and mouth

3 Large scissors for cutting fabric

4 Tweezers/cuticle scissors for working with small socks, to help turn the fabric inside out, or to help when stuffing

5 Small, pointed scissors for seam ripping

6 Erasable marking pen

7 Two needles

8 One blue cotton/wool sock for body (knee-high socks will make a taller frog) and one green sock for mouth (green sock should be much more stretchy than the blue sock)

9 Two larger buttons for the eyes and two smaller black beads for the pupils

10 Lace or ribbon for skirt

11 Stuffing (not shown in photo)

3 Turn right side out through the hole. Use tweezers/cuticle scissors to shape the eyes.

2 Turn the body inside out and close seams with backstitches. Leave a hole in between the feet large enough to turn the piece right side out and fill with stuffing.

1 Mark the blue sock as illustrated above and cut out pieces. You will cut the entire body of the frog from one sock with the heel as the mouth of the frog. A knee-high sock will enable you to make a taller frog.

I'm a baby sock frog!

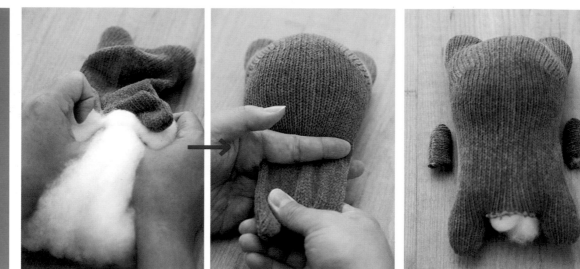

4 First, use two small balls of stuffing to fill
   the eyes. Next, use a large ball of stuffing
   for the head. Pack the eyes and the head
   stuffing tightly to achieve a full, round look.
   Pull the remaining sock down and compact
   the stuffing to ensure the head is nice and
   round.

5 Use small amounts of stuffing
   to fill the legs and arms. Next,
   fill the body area beneath the
   head with some flat-shaped
   stuffing. Mold the body carefully
   to ensure there are no gaps
   between the pieces of stuffing.
   If you need to adjust the
   proportions, remove stuffing
   and refill with correct amount.

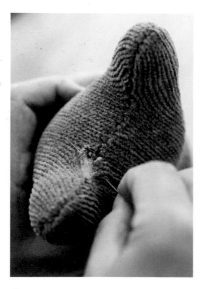

6 Stitch seam together with
   backstitches.

7 Sew the arms onto the
   body. Make sure they are
   symmetrically positioned
   on each side.

8 For the eyes, use cross stitches to sew on the white buttons. Sew the black beads on top of the white buttons to form the pupils.

9 Draw a straight line on each side of the heel of the green sock and cut the piece out. The edges of the piece will curl naturally because of the elasticity.

10 Pull the piece over the head and position it level with where the mouth should be. The curled edge will create a big, happy smile. On either side of face, use small stitches to attach mouth to head.

11 To make the skirt, sew the lace into a circle and position it above the legs.

Happy Monkey

BASIC 4 — Daniel's Classroom Tips

⊕ This monkey requires a cotton sock with a color block around the toes. The color block will become the hair of the monkey and a cotton sock will give the face a smooth finish.

⊕ I like the contrast of the head and the body, so I chose not to stuff the body too full. The contrast of a big, round head and a lean body makes this little monkey especially cute.

✖ Materials and Tools

1 Black thread for eyes
2 Dark brown thread for ears and body
3 White thread for head
4 Large scissors for cutting fabric
5 Tweezers/cuticle scissors for working with small socks, to help turn the fabric inside out, or to help when stuffing
6 Small, pointed scissors for seam ripping
7 Erasable marking pen
8 Two needles
9 Two ¾ inch (2 cm) diameter black beads for eyes
10 One pair of flowered socks
11 One white cotton sock with a gray sole
12 Stuffing (not shown in photo)

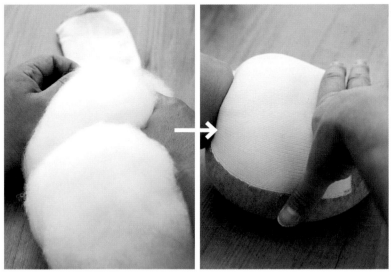

1 Turn the white sock inside out and trim the rough edges of the fabric where the white and gray colors meet. This will ensure the face has a smooth appearance.

2 Mold a large amount of stuffing into a ball. Push stuffing all the way to the toe keeping in mind that the color block will become the monkey's hair. Shape the head into a nice round form and push the stuffing in where the eyes will be. This will create indents for the eyes.

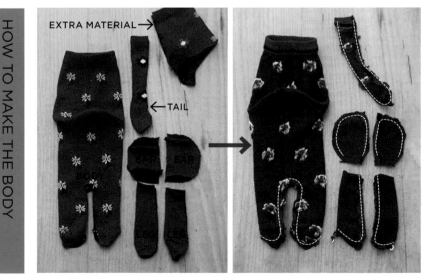

EXTRA MATERIAL →

← TAIL

3 Cut off the extra sock leg and cuff and sew the seam together with running stitches.

4 Take one flowered sock and cut a thin strip from the middle of the toe upwards to make the legs. Each leg should be approximately 3⅛ inches (8 cm) long.

From the other flowered sock, cut the monkey's tail from the cuff and back portion of the sock. Cut two ear pieces and two arms from the sole of the sock. Always outline shapes before cutting.

Turn pieces inside out and stitch seams together.

5 Fill the ears, arms, and tail with stuffing. Use small balls of stuffing to fill the legs. Do not stuff the body too full, but add extra stuffing at the heel, which will become the monkey's bottom. With a full, round bottom, the monkey can be placed in a sitting position.

6 Use the erasable marker to outline the eyes, mouth, ears, and eyebrows.

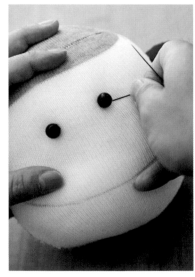

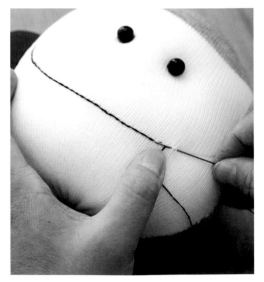

7 Stitch the ears (stuffed in step 5) onto head. Make sure they are symmetrically positioned on each side.

8 Sew on the two black beads as the eyes. To set the eyes into the face, pull the thread taught to create a dimple in the stuffing.

9 With a double thread, use running stitches to outline the mouth.

10 To outline the eyebrows, use running stitches.

11 Attach the body and head with ladder stitches. It is easier to position the body and secure the head tightly if you hold the monkey upside down.

12 Sew arms onto body making sure they are symmetrically positioned on each side.

13 Lastly, attach the tail to the body. Now you have completed your sock monkey!

Miss Mini

BASIC 5 — Daniel's Classroom Tips

○ Use a baby sock to make Miss Mini. Be sure not stuff her head too full so you have enough room left over to make the rest of her body with the same sock.

○ You can decorate her any way you prefer, but keep it simple since she is so tiny. Buttons, beads, and ribbons are all good options.

✕ Materials and Tools

1 White thread for body
2 Black thread for eyes
3 Large scissors for cutting fabric
4 Tweezers/cuticle scissors for working with small socks, to help turn the fabric inside out, or to help when stuffing
5 Small, pointed scissors for seam ripping
6 Red pencil to color cheeks
7 Erasable marking pen
8 Two needles
9 Two ⅛ inch (4mm) diameter black beads for eyes
10 One baby sock with a lace or frilly cuff
11 Stuffing (not shown in photo)

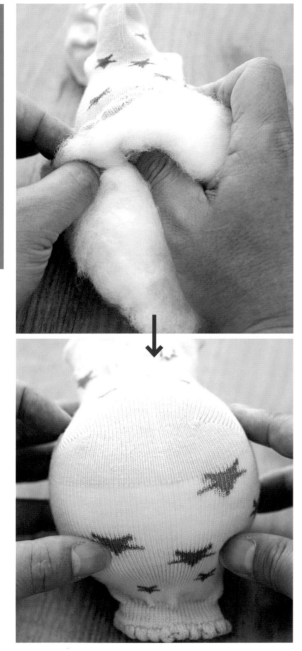

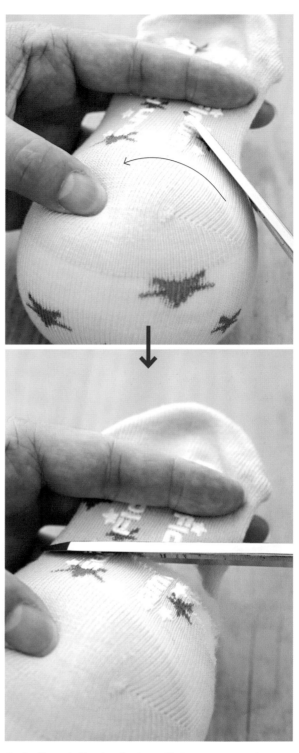

1   Take a small amount of filling, mold into a ball shape, and push the ball to the heel of the sock. The color block of the heel will become the face. Leave 2–2.5 inches (6–7 cm) of room below the head area to make the body. Leave ½–1 inch (2–3 cm) of cuff above the head area to make the ears.

2   Pull sock flat and trim off the extra sock material along the head area. Cut an even curve so that the head will be have a nice, round shape.

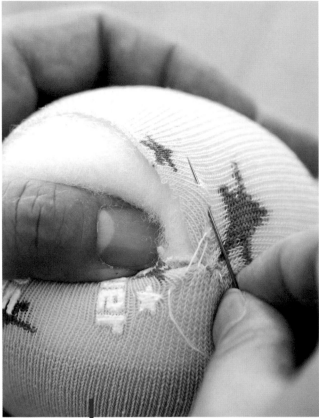

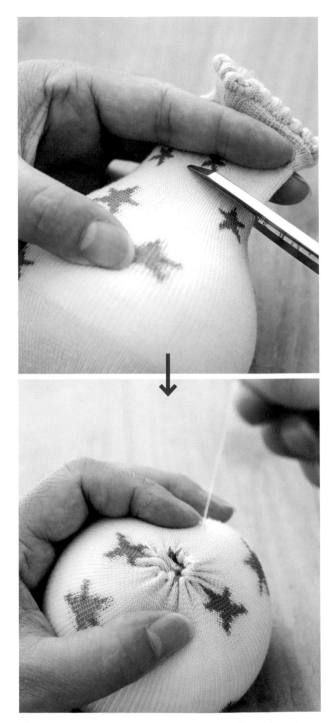

3 Because the sock is small, push the filling inside the sock and close up the opening with dense, tight slip stitches. Take care to stitch the opening in a way that will result in a smooth, round finish.

4 On the other side of the head, pull sock flat and cut off remaining sock in a straight line. Seal the opening with straight stitches and pull the thread taut to close up the hole.

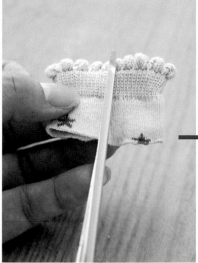

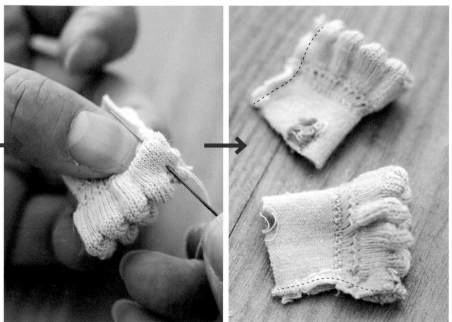

5 Cut the cuff remnant in two equal parts. Turn each inside out and use backstitches to sew the edges together.

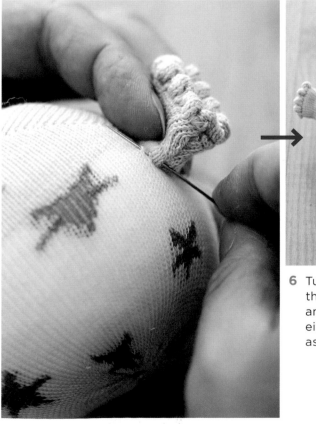

6 Turn right side out, fold the uneven edges inside, and attach the cuffs on either side of the head as ears.

Miss Mini makes me see stars!

7 Use the erasable marking pen to outline the eyes and smile.

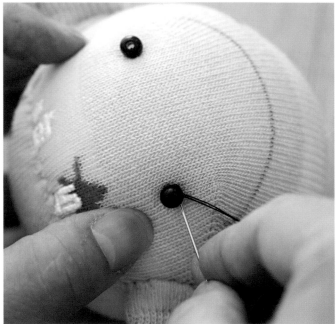

8 Sew on the beads as the eyes and hide the knots under each bead.

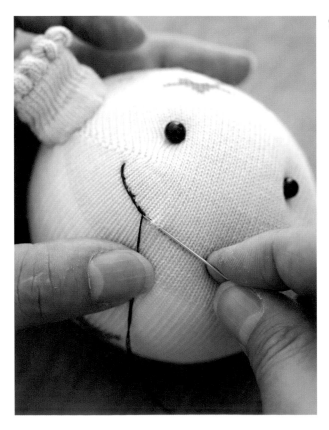

9 Use split running stitches to outline the smile.

10 Use colored pencil to add pink cheeks.

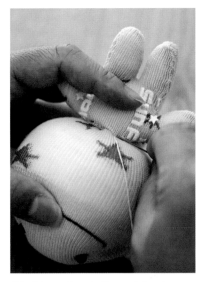

13 Turn the doll upside down and securely attach the body to the head with ladder stitches.

11 Draw the body shape on the leftover toe portion. Turn the sock inside out and cut out body shape. Stitch seams together.

12 Turn right side out and use tweezers or cuticle scissors to fill in the arms and legs, and then fill the rest of the body.

Miss Mini and I are best friends!

Baby Bunny

BASIC 6 Daniel's Classroom Tips

● You may choose any color scarf for your sock bunny. I chose the contrasting color to give the light blue bunny a warm, cozy feel.

● It is important to choose thick baby socks for this bunny. A single color sock is preferable because it highlights the soft texture. To give the rabbit a chubby face and body, use plenty of stuffing.

✖ Materials and Tools

1. Black thread for eyes
2. White thread for body and legs
3. Large scissors for cutting fabric
4. Tweezers/cuticle scissors for working with small socks, to help turn the fabric inside out, or to help when stuffing
5. Small, pointed scissors for seam ripping
6. Erasable marking pen
7. Red pencil to color cheeks
8. Two needles
9. Two 1/2 inch (6 mm) diameter black beads for eyes
10. One black button for nose
11. Two brown buttons for body
12. One pair of single-colored baby socks made from thick wool or cotton
13. One striped sock for scarf
14. Stuffing (not shown in photo)

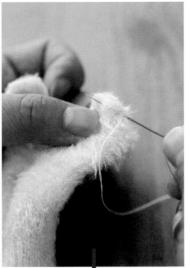

1 Begin at the middle of the toe and cut up 2 inches (5 cm) to the heel of both socks. One sock will become the head and ears, the other will become the body and legs.

EAR
EAR
HEAD
BODY
LEG
LEG

3 Turn the socks inside out and use backstitches to sew the seams together.

2 Round the toe sections of one of the socks with your scissors; these will become the feet.

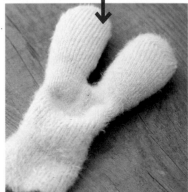

4 Form stuffing into round tubes and fill both ears. Make sure they match in shape and size.

Baby Bunny **89**

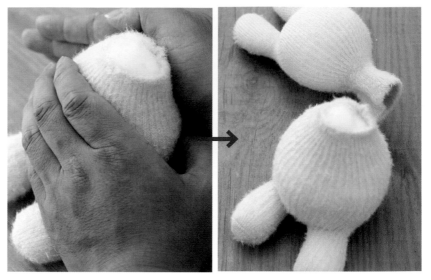

5 For the head, use plenty of stuffing and mold into a ball. Leave 2 inches (5 cm) of material at the bottom to be used for the arms.

6 Take the other sock and fill legs with equal amounts of stuffing. For the body, use more stuffing than was used for the head and form it into a pear shape. Use very little stuffing between the legs and the body so that the legs can move around easily.

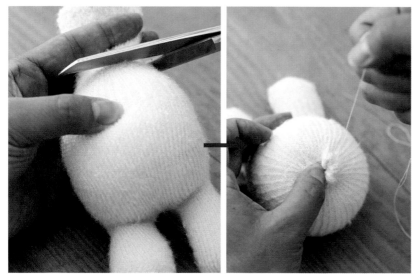

7 Below the head, cut off the remaining 2 inches (5 cm) of material and save for the arms. Use running stitches to seal off the opening.

8 After sealing off the opening, continue with the same thread and stitch the back of the head to the body. Line up the back of the head with the lower back so the head tilts back slightly. Secure with a strong knot.

9 Use ladder stitches to attach the rest of the head to the body.

11 To make the arms, cut the cuff in two equal parts and round one end of each arm with your scissors.

12 Turn the arm pieces inside out and use backstitches to sew seams together. Fill tubes with stuffing, but leave some space at the end.

10 Push the body down so the center of gravity is at the lower region and use the legs to help the bunny sit flat.

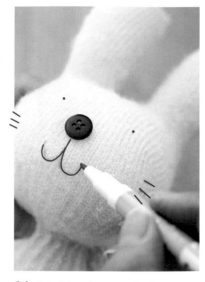

13 Use backstitches to attach the arms to where the head meets the body. Make sure they are evenly positioned.

14 Position button in the center of the face and use the erasable marking pen to draw the eyes, mouth, and whiskers.

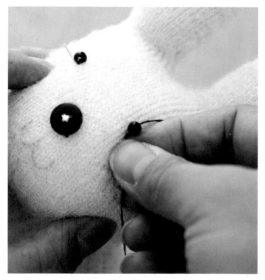

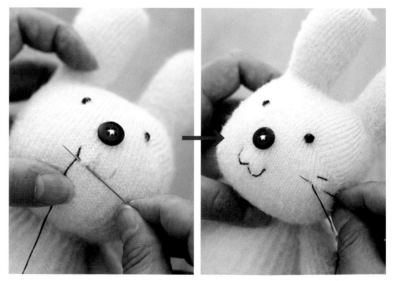

15 Use white thread to sew on button; hide knot underneath. Use black thread to sew on the beads as the eyes.

16 Use split running stitches to outline the mouth and whiskers. Sew and tie off each part separately so you won't have to re-do the whole area if you make a mistake on one part.

17 Mark the location of the buttons on the body. Sew on the buttons with cross stitches.

18 Use colored pencil to add pink cheeks.

You can also use leftover scraps to make different scarves.

19 Tie the striped sock around the neck of the bunny as a scarf. Position knot at the back.

Mrs. Honey

ADVANCED

1

Daniel's
Classroom Tips

○ The secret to making a cute bee is a round, chubby body and a smiling face tilted upward. Be sure to use plenty of stuffing in the body and head, and mold into smooth, round shapes.

○ Make sure to fill in the small corners with tweezers or small scissors to give the bee an overall fullness.

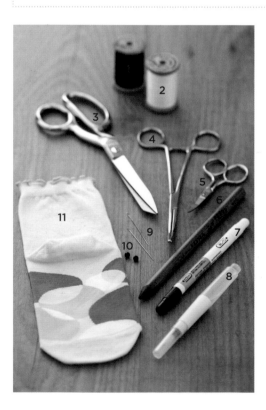

⊗ **Materials and Tools**

1 Black thread for eyes

2 White thread for body, legs, and wings

3 Large scissors for cutting fabric

4 Tweezers/cuticle scissors for working with small socks, to help turn the fabric inside out, or to help when stuffing

5 Small, pointed scissors for seam ripping

6 Red pencil to color cheeks

7 Erasable marking pen

8 Water-based erasing pen

9 Two needles

10 Two ½ inch (6 mm) diameter black beads for eyes

11 One children's sock with a frilly cuff

12 Stuffing (not shown in photo)

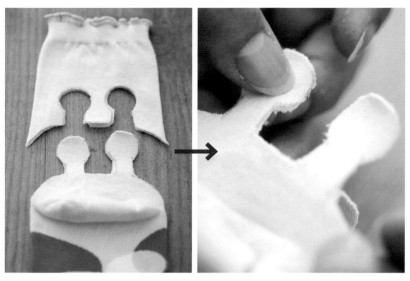

1 Turn the sock inside out and cut ¼ inch (0.5mm) off the toe to form a hole. Just above the heel, about ⅓ of the way down the sock from the cuff, outline the ears.

2 Making sure the ears are the same size, cut along the ear pattern.

3 Cut remaining cuff of sock into 3 pieces. Cut the cuff ¾ inch (1.5 cm) deep to make the necklace. The middle part will become the wings, and the areas outside the ears will become the legs.

4 Fold leg material in half. Cut off the extra material and make legs into a tube shape with one end rounded.

5 Fold the material for the wings in half. Outline the shape of the wings and cut pieces out.

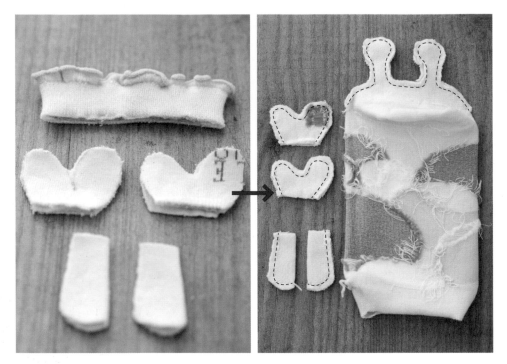

6 Turn the pieces inside out and use backstitches to sew the seams together.

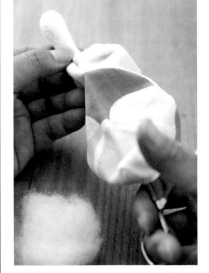

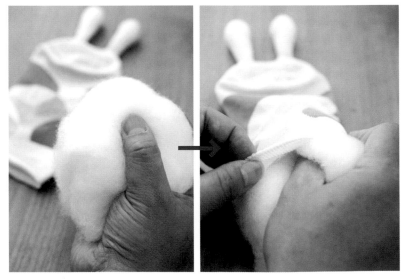

7 Stuff a small amount of filling into each ear and mold into the shape of a tear drop.

8 Take a large amount of stuffing, form into a ball, and fill head.

9 Pull the sock beneath the head tight to compact the stuffing into the head.

10 Take 2-3 times more stuffing than was used for the head. Shape into a ball and fill body.

11 Once finished, mold each section. The head should be nice and round and the body should be larger than the head and pear shaped.

12 Use running stitches to close up the hole at the bottom of the body.

13 Turn the legs and wings to the right side with small tweezers or cuticle scissors.

14 Stuff the legs and wings making sure all corners are filled in to give them a nice rounded form.

15 Sew the seams of the wings together with dense split running stitches.

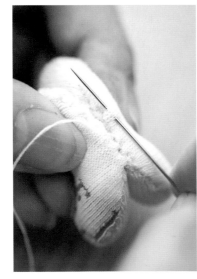

16 Attach the two wings together. Pull thread tight with each stitch so that the wings stand up closely together.

17 Position wings in the middle of the body, slightly down from where the head and body connect. It is critical to find the right location in order to give the bee the correct look. Stitch the wings onto position.

18 Attach legs to the body with split running stitches.

19 Place the frilly cuff around the neck to make the necklace. Below it, measure in ⅝ inch (1.5 cm) from the side of the body.

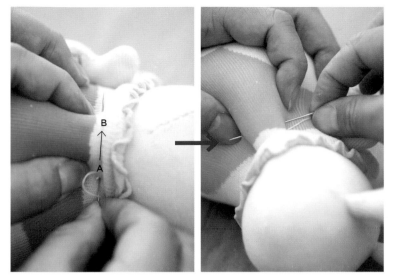

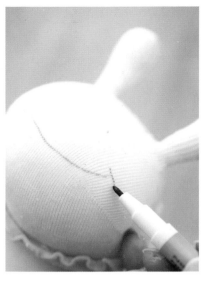

20 Use backstitches from point A to point B to create the arms. Each arm should be ⅝ inch (1.5 cm) thick. Pull thread tight with each stitch to shape the arm. Continue sewing until the arm is ¾ inch (2 cm) long.

21 Use erasable marking pen to outline the position of the eyes and mouth.

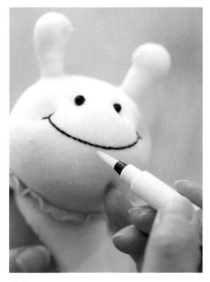

22 Sew beads on as the eyes. Use split running stitches to sew along the mouth.

23 Use colored pencil to add pink cheeks.

24 In hot and humid weather, the marking may not disappear automatically. Use an erasing pen to remove the lines.

Penny Penguin

ADVANCED
2

Daniel's Classroom Tips

🔘 You can avoid making a lumpy-looking doll by following these steps: Before stuffing your doll, estimate how much filling is needed for the head and body. Next, mold the stuffing into one shape. Finish by pushing the shaped ball of stuffing into the head and body of the doll all at once. This technique will help to make smooth and cuddly dolls.

🔘 Use longer socks like knee socks for this project.

🔘 Decorate your penguin any way you like (I used a bowtie and a felted flower).

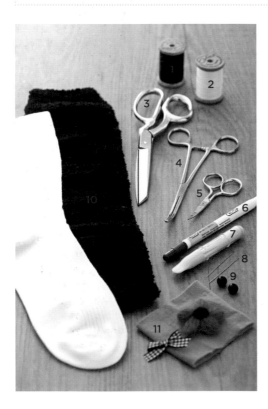

✖ Materials and Tools

1 Black thread for eyes
2 White thread for body and legs
3 Large scissors for cutting fabric
4 Tweezers/cuticle scissors for working with small socks, to help turn the fabric inside out, or to help when stuffing
5 Small, pointed scissors for seam ripping
6 Erasable marking pen
7 Marking chalk/pen
8 Two needles
9 Two $^3/_8$ inch (10 mm) diameter black beads for eyes
10 One black terry cloth knee sock and one white cotton knee sock
11 Orange colored scrap of fabric for beak
12 One bow tie or ribbon and one felted flower
11 Stuffing (not shown in photo)

1 Cut 2 inches (5 cm) below the sock's toe creating a round edge.

2 Turn the sock inside out and close the seam using the backstitch. Use any color thread. The terry cloth will hide the stitches.

3 Use the leftover part of the sock to make the penguin wings. Round edges with scissors.

4 Use the erasable marking pen to outline the beak on the orange material. The beak should be around 2 inches (5cm) long and 1½ inches (4cm) wide.

5 Turn the pieces inside out and use the backstitch to sew seams together.

6 Mold a large amount of stuffing into an elongated form about 8-10 inches (20-25 cm) tall and 6 inches (15 cm) wide. Pack the stuffing tightly into body. If there is too much or not enough stuffing, you'll need to pull it out, reshape a new amount, and refill.

7 Cut off the remaining sock. Close the opening with running stitches and pull thread tight.

9 Use the chalk to outline the belly area of the penguin.

8 Turn beak and wings right side out and fill with stuffing.

10 Hold and stretch out the heel part of the white cotton sock.

11 Match the white sock to the marked belly area of the black sock. Position the heel of the white sock at the bottom of the body. Sew the white sock to the black sock, pulling the edges of the white sock tight so it lays flat.

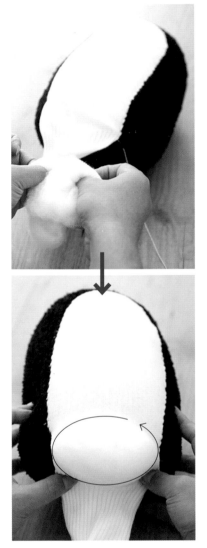

12 To make the feet, stuff the heel part of the white sock at the bottom of the body and form it into a football shape.

13 Pull the leftover sock cuff toward the back to cover half of the bottom part of the body. Cut off the remaining cuff.

14 Tuck and fold the edge of the white sock to hide the seam then stitch it onto the black sock.

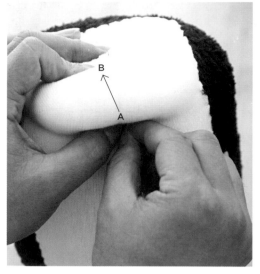

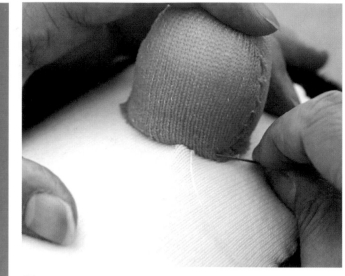

15 Squeeze the heel part in the middle. Stitch from point A to point B and pull the thread tight to form a convex shape on each side. Repeat this stitch a few times to create the space between the two feet.

17 Use the backstitch to sew the beak onto the body. While sewing, try to push the seam in about ⅛ inch (0.1 cm) to hide it.

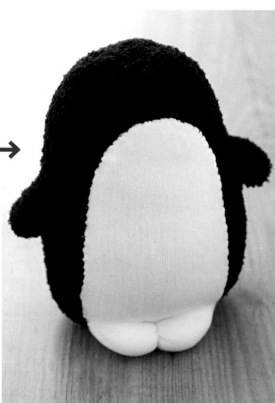

16 Use the backstitch to sew the wings to the body. Position the wings midway between the head and feet at the same height on opposite sides.

My tummy is so big I can barely see my feet!

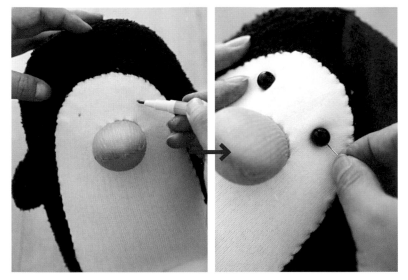

18 Mark the position of the eyes and sew the beads on with black thread. Try to hide the knot beneath the eye.

19 To highlight the opening of the beak, use black thread and pull it tight from point A to point B. It should sink into the stuffing.

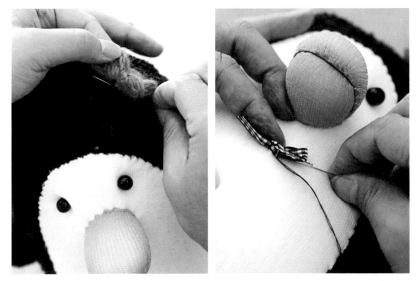

20 Sew decorative pieces onto the penguin. I chose a flower for its hair and a bow tie or ribbon for its tuxedo. You can choose whatever you like!

The Peeking Squirrel

ADVANCED

3

Daniel's
Classroom Tips

- Outlining the eyes, whiskers, and mouth in the correct location is the key to a lifelike face.
- Use baby socks with a very fluffy texture in a light, solid color for this little squirrel.

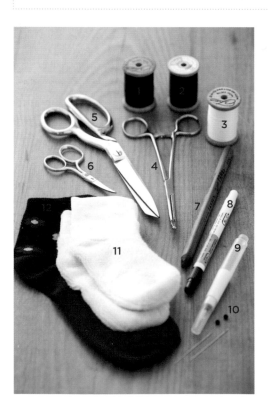

✕ Materials and Tools

1 Black thread for eyes
2 Brown thread for whiskers and to attach acorn
3 White thread for ears and seams
4 Tweezers/cuticle scissors for working with small socks, to help turn the fabric inside out, or to help when stuffing
5 Large scissors for cutting fabric
6 Small, pointed scissors for seam ripping
7 Red pencil to color nose
8 Erasable marking pen
9 Pen eraser (optional) to remove any markings on the material
10 Two ⅛ inch (4 mm) diameter black beads for eyes
11 One pair of vanilla or light yellow baby socks with fluffy terry cloth inside, elastic cuffs, and a color block at heel
12 One dark brown and terracotta colored sock for an acorn
13 Stuffing (not shown in photo)

1 Turn one baby sock inside out, and take a fist size amount of stuffing and fill toe area. Form into a long oval shape with a flat bottom so the body will stand up.

2 For the head, mold a smaller amount of stuffing into a pear shape and fill heel area. Make sure the heel color block faces up; it will become the face.

3 Cut 1¼ inches (3 cm) from the cuff; this will become the ears.

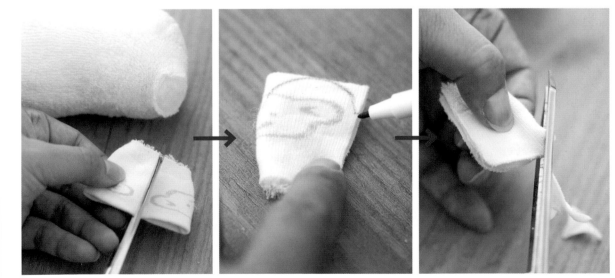

4 Cut the cuff into two equal parts. Use the erasable marking pen to outline the shape of the ears and create round corners with scissors. Keeping the cuff intact, trim the edges. Turn ears inside out and use backstitches to sew seams together.

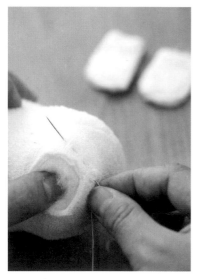

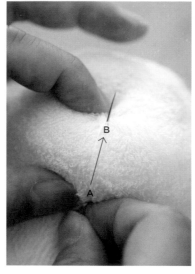

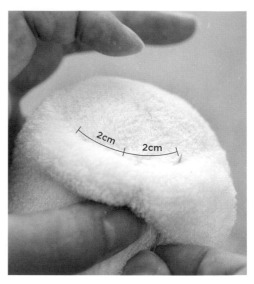

5 Close the opening on the body with running stitches. Make sure the color block is on top, as it will become the face.

6 About ¾ inch (2 cm) below the heel color block, pinch a section of the stuffing ⅝ of an inch (1.5 cm) thick. Stitch from point A to point B a few times and pull thread tight to make an indentation.

7 For the arm, continue to hold ⅝ of an inch (1.5 cm) thick of stuffing to the left of the indentation. Backstitch densely from top to bottom about ⅜ inch (2 cm) long and pull thread tight. Repeat on the right side to make other arm.

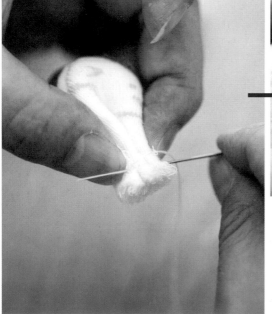

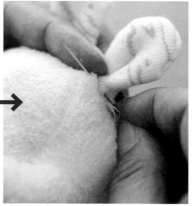

8 Turn stitched ears right side out and pinch the bottom to create ear dimples. Hold in place and sew the ears onto the head.

We squirrels come in all shapes and sizes!

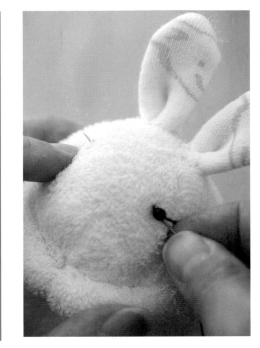

9 Mark location of the eyes and sew on beads.

11 Mark location of the whiskers.

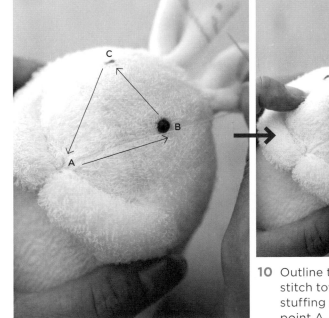

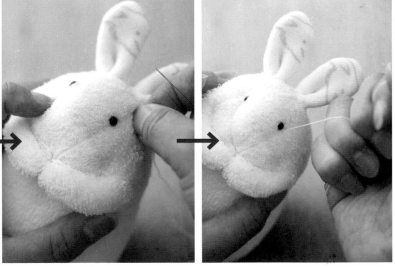

10 Outline the nose area. From the middle of the arms (A), stitch towards the left eye (B). Hide thread under the stuffing and exit at other eye (C). Stitch from point C to point A. Pull thread tight between A-B and C-A to make indentations defining the nose area. Repeat stitches if indentations are not deep enough.

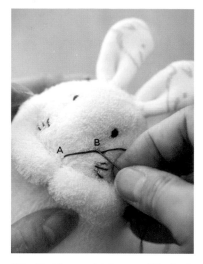

12 Outline whiskers with dark brown thread. Double the thread to make them thicker. Use dark brown thread to highlight nose. Sew from point A to point B to form a V shape ⅝ inch (1.5 cm) long on each side.

13 Color nose area pink to give the squirrel an extra cute look.

14 Turn one sock inside out and fill with stuffing, about ⅔ size of the body. Mold stuffing into an oval shape resembling a tail.

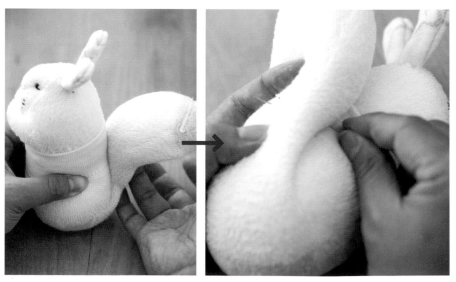

15 Pull tail onto the body and secure with the elastic cuff. Leave a gap in the stuffing between the tail and body.

16 Push tail upright and stitch the end of the tail to the body. Use the needle to go through the stuffing with each stitch. The tail should be held upright against the body without flopping around.

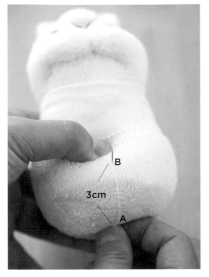

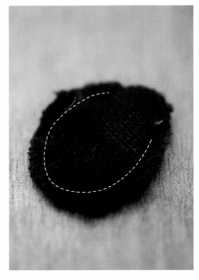

17 Use running stitches to sew from point A to point B, about 1¼ inches (3 cm) long. Repeat stitches and pull thread tight to make an indentation separating the feet.

18 Turn the dark brown and terracotta colored sock inside out. Cut out an oval shape. The main color for the acorn should be dark brown.

19 Use backstitches to sew seams together. Leave a small opening for the stuffing.

I like acorns too!

20 Stuff the acorn and close the opening with black thread. Do not cut the thread after sewing. Leave 2 inches (5 cm) of thread and use to attach the acorn to the hands.

Cheshire Cat

ADVANCED 4

Daniel's Classroom Tips

⊙ Help the cat's big grin stand out by using light colored socks for the head and body and a dark colored thread for the facial expression and details.

⊙ Because you will use almost every bit of this pair of socks, you'll need to plan carefully. If you make an error, you may need to use an additional sock.

✕ Materials and Tools

1 White thread for body
2 Black thread for eyes and teeth
3 Brown thread for nose
4 Large scissors for cutting fabric
5 Tweezers/cuticle scissors for working with small socks, to help turn the fabric inside out, or to help when stuffing
6 Small, pointed scissors for seam ripping
7 Erasable marking pen
8 Two needles
9 One pair of thick striped wool socks
10 Brown scrap material
11 Stuffing (not shown in photo)

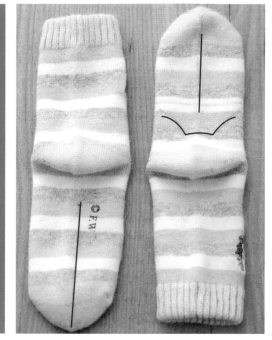

1   Position and trace the pattern onto socks. The left sock becomes the front legs and the right sock will be the back legs and head.

3   First, shape two small balls of stuffing and fill each ear. Next, take a large amount of stuffing and shape it into ball. Tightly pack the ball of stuffing into the head.

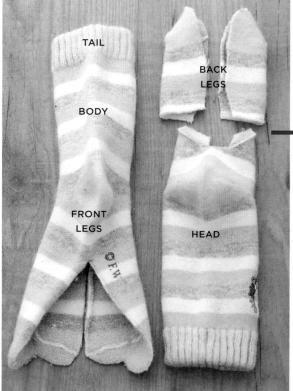

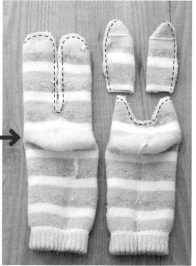

2   Cut the socks according to the pattern and turn them inside out. Use backstitches to sew the front legs, back legs and the head.

Cheshire Cat   **113**

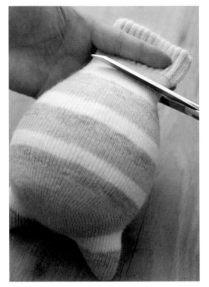  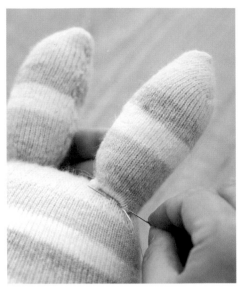

4 Cut 1½ inches (4 cm) off of the remaining sock (this will become the tail). Sew the opening shut using running stitches.

5 Mold the head into a ball shape. The color block on the heel, which will become the outline of the face, should to be about half of the head area so there is room for the wide grin.

6 Fill the front legs with stuffing and then mold into cone shapes. Leave the area where the legs attach to the body free of stuffing so they can move easily.

7 For the body, mold stuffing into an oval shape and fill body cavity. If you skimped and need to add more stuffing, take it all out, re-mold and refill. Use running stitches to close opening.

Wool socks make us warm & cozy!

8 Use the leftover cuff piece from step 4 and cut it in half. This will become the tail.

9 If the cuff has a double layer, rip the seam open and unfold second layer.

10 Fold piece in half with wrong side facing out. Round corners with scissors and stitch seams together leaving an opening at the bottom.

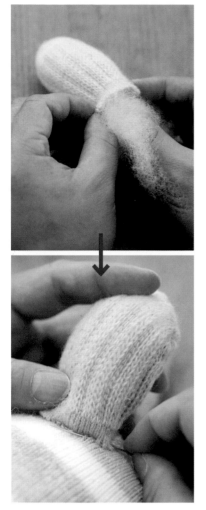

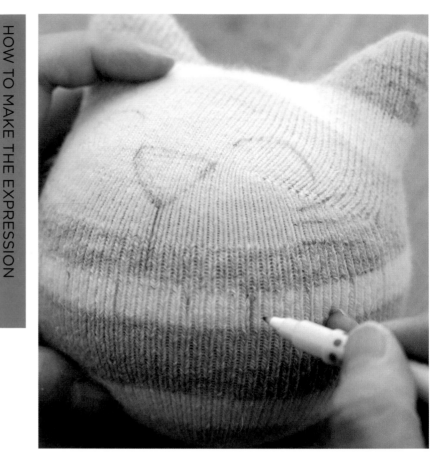

11 Mold the tail into a cone
    shape, then fill it with
    stuffing and attach it
    to the body.

12 Draw the outline for the eyes, nose, and mouth.
    Position the eyes and nose on the sock color
    block area and then mold the face so the nose
    and mouth jut out.

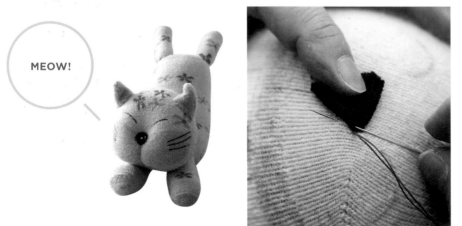

MEOW!

13 Cut the brown fabric scrap
    into a two-layered triangle.
    Position it to the face and
    review the position of the
    eyes and mouth, then stitch
    onto the nose.

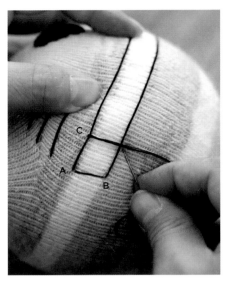

14 Use a split running stitch to outline the eyes and whiskers. For a thicker line, double the thread.

15 For the top of the mouth, use a split running stitch to sew a straight line (tracing the sock's stripe) from point A to point B. Repeat this for the lower line of the mouth.

16 For the teeth, first sew from point A to point B. At point B, insert needle under stuffing and pull out at point C. Repeat steps to outline all of the teeth.

17 Hide the knot under the nose and pull the needle out at the bottom of the nose near the teeth. Sew a straight line from point A to point B.

18 Use ladder stitches to sew the head and the body together. Tilt the head so it's looking up and then begin stitching. Make sure to sew through plenty of stuffing with each stitch to securely attach the head and body.

Striped Elephant

ADVANCED
5

Daniel's Classroom Tips

⊕ Positioning the elephant's head, so that she's looking up at her trunk, makes her look really cute!
⊕ Striped socks work well to highlight the elephant's smile.
⊕ Be sure to mold the trunk carefully.

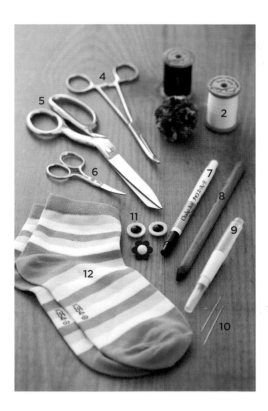

⊗ Materials and Tools

1 Black thread for eyes
2 White thread for ears and feet
3 One colorful wool ball for the trunk
4 Tweezers/cuticle scissors (helps turn the fabric inside out and to stuff small socks)
5 Large scissors for cutting fabric
6 Small, pointed scissors for seam ripping
7 Erasable marking pen
8 Red pencil to color cheeks
9 Erasable marking pen
10 Two needles
11 Two buttons (black & white colored buttons work well) for eyes and one flower shaped button for decoration.
12 One pair of colorful striped socks
13 Stuffing (not shown in photo)

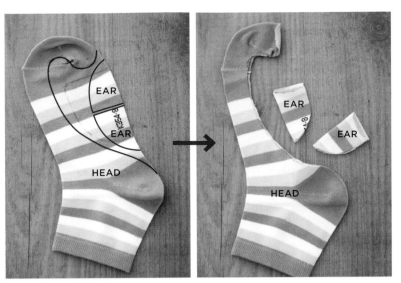

1   First trace the pattern onto the sock (the head and ears). Next cut out the pattern making sure to cut round corners for the ears and trunk. The color block of the heel will become the elephant's face.

2   Turn the sock pieces inside out and use backstitches to sew seams together.

For a correct body-head ratio select the right amount of stuffing.

Body: Use the second sock for the body. Take a large ball of stuffing (3-4 times larger than your fist) and pack it into the heel. Flatten the bottom so the elephant can stand. Fill the rest of sock with another ball of stuffing (half as much as before).

Head & Trunk: Fill the tip of trunk with a small ball of stuffing then fill the main part of the trunk with another ball of stuffing (size of a fist). Mold evenly so the end of the trunk is thinner and reaches upward. Form a smooth ball of stuffing and fill head.

Ears: Fill ears with small amounts of stuffing and leave ends empty.

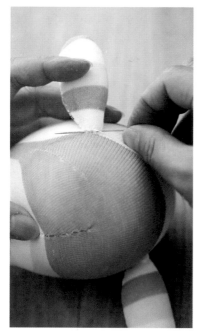

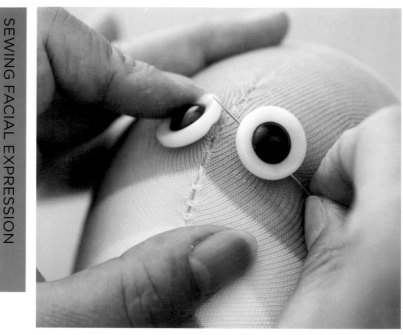

4 Close the opening on the head with running stitches. Sew the ears on each side of the head using ladder stitches.

5 First, mark the location of the eyes. Hide the thread underneath the button and sew on both the eyes.

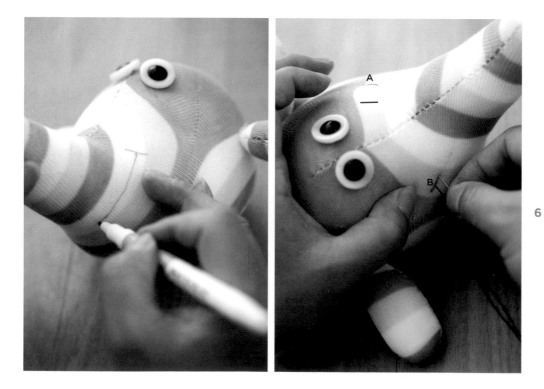

6 Use the erasable marking pen to outline the position of the mouth under the trunk. Next, draw the A and B lines as illustrated. Then with split running stitches sew line A.

7 Pull thread along mouth line from A to B. Use running stitches to sew line B and pull the thread tight. The thread should follow the curve of the mouth line.

8 Stuff a smaller amount of filling on top of the main body and flatten.

9 Fold the cuff down and mark the center point.

10 Insert the needle below the center point and pull thread up the center to the top of the body where you'll start the next stitch. Sew back and forth twice between the two points. Pull the thread tight each time so that the thread sinks into the stuffing to form the front legs of the elephant.

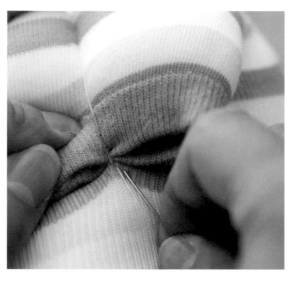

11 Repeat step 10 twice. You should have a clear, concave line separating the front legs.

12 Finish the last stitch at the center point of the legs. Pull the knot tight to pronounce the shape of the legs.

13 Tilting the head upward while sewing, stitch the head onto the body with ladder stitches.

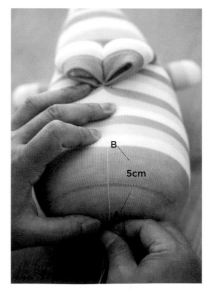

14 Insert needle at point A. Sew through stuffing and exit at point B (about 2 inches from point A). Pull thread tight so it sinks into stuffing and forms wrinkles.

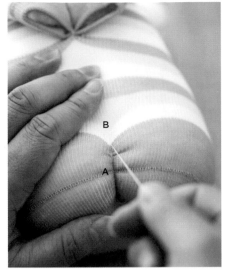

15 Repeat step 14 twice. You should have a clear, concave line separating the back legs.

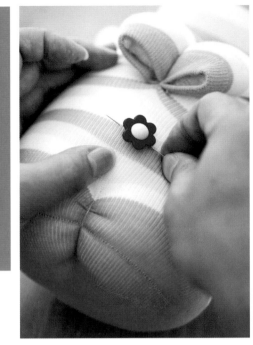

16 To give your elephant additional flair, sew on a decorative button or other items in the middle of the tummy.

17 Use ladder stitches to attach the fluffy ball on the tip of the trunk.

18 Add pink cheeks with the colored pencil.

Step by Step   Zen Tiger

ADVANCED
6

Daniel's Classroom Tips

⊗ Use terry cloth socks to give the tiger a fluffy coat. Cotton socks will be too smooth a texture for this big, furry cat.

⊗ To add energy to the tiger's eyes, use striped wooden buttons. Black plastic or metal buttons will not work as well.

⊗ Materials and Tools

1 White thread for body
2 Black thread for eyes
3 Brown thread for nose
4 Large scissors for cutting fabric
5 Tweezers/cuticle scissors for working with small socks, to help turn the fabric inside out, or to help when stuffing
6 Small, pointed scissors for seam ripping
7 Erasable marking pen
8 Two needles
9 Two wooden buttons and two white buttons for eyes
10 One pair of terry cloth knee socks
11 One terracotta-colored scrap of sock for nose
12 Stuffing (not shown in photo)

1   Mold a fist size amount of stuffing into a ball and fill toe of the first sock to make the mouth. Next take twice as much stuffing and fill in the area behind the mouth to make the head. Shape the two portions of stuffing so they connect smoothly.

 TIP   **Before stuffing, turn the sock inside out and trim loose threads. The black and white stripes should be nice and clean.**

2   Cut off remaining 8 inches (20 cm) of sock. This will become the tail and ears. Close seam with running stitches.

3 Cut up the middle of the heel and cuff off the other sock, about 3⅝ inches (9 cm). Use the heel for the front paws and the cuff for back paws. Use the leftover scrap from step 2 for the tail and ears.

4 Trim rounded corners on tops of ears.

5 Turn pieces inside out and use backstitches to close seams.

6 Before stuffing, trim loose threads to make the strips look clean.

7 Cut a tiny hole in the heel to add stuffing. You only need a small opening.

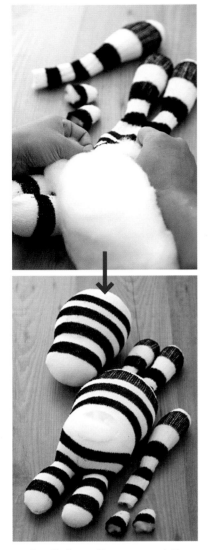

9   Use the toe area of the sock as the tiger's mouth, and mark the position of the eyes. Pinch 2-3 stripes and stitch them together in the middle. Sew through enough stuffing with each stitch in order to create the shape of the eye area. Mark the location of the eyes and mouth as illustrated.

8   Stuff the tail, ears, and the front and back legs. Shape the parts while stuffing to give them a nice rounded form. Stitch opening in heel closed.

10 Symmetrically sew the ears onto each side of the head.

12 Pushing the edges inward to hide the fringe, use backstitches to sew two sides of the nose onto the face. Leave one side open and fill with stuffing so nose is round and full. Stitch opening closed.

11 For the nose, draw a triangle 2 inches (5 cm) long on each side. Cut out the double-layered (very important) triangle and round corners.

13 Outline whiskers and mouth of the tiger.

Keep on sewing!

14 Enter needle at point A and hide knot under the nose. Pull thread tightly across to point B so it sinks into the stuffing. Stitch from point B to point A, back and forth a couple of times.

16 Stitch head to body. Pull stitches tight to secure the head firmly in place.

15 Use split running stitches to outline whiskers. Sew on eyes with cross stitches using the white buttons for pupils on top of the wooden buttons.

17 Stitch tail onto the back of tiger. Leave end of tail free of stuffing so it can move easily.

Best Friend's Sheep Dog

ADVANCED 7 Daniel's Classroom Tips

- Dense, long hair on the head is the key characteristic of this sheep dog. Spread yarn evenly and use a good amount.
- Take care to keep the white yarn clean while making the dog. You can also use black yarn.

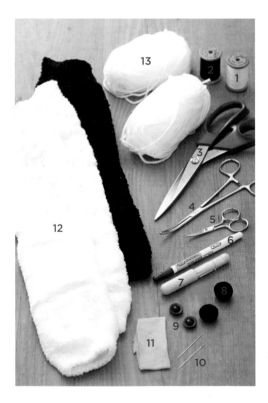

⊗ Materials and Tools

1. Black thread for eyes
2. White thread for body and legs
3. Large scissors for cutting fabric
4. Tweezers/cuticle scissors for working with small socks, to help turn the fabric inside out, or to help when stuffing
5. Small pointed scissors for seam ripping
6. Erasable marking pen
7. Chalk to mark lines on the dark colored material
8. Two black woolly balls for nose
9. Two black buttons (preferably with a raised center as used here) or beads for eyes
10. Two needles
11. One pink-colored scrap of sock for tongue
12. Two pair of terry cloth tube socks (one in white and one in black). It is best to use fluffy knee socks without heels.
13. Two balls of white yarn for long hair
14. Stuffing (not shown in photo)

BODY

1   At an angle, cut off one of the corners of the toe of a white sock. Do not cut into a round shape; the dog's head should be oval.

HEAD

BODY

LEG

LEG

LEG

LEG

2   Cut other white sock in half between the toe and cuff. Then cut each part again in the middle, about 6 inches (15 cm) in length. Round corners to make front and back legs.

3   Cut pink scrap into an inch (2 cm) square. Be sure it is double layered. Round two of the corners. From the wrong side, stitch three of the seams together.

That's my older brother.

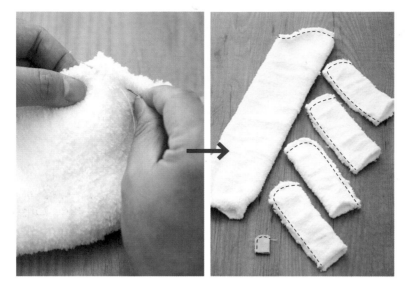

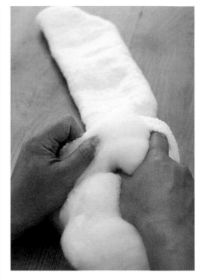

4 Use backstitches to sew the seams together.

5 To form the head, turn sock right side out and fill with a large ball of stuffing, about 3-4 times the size of your fist.

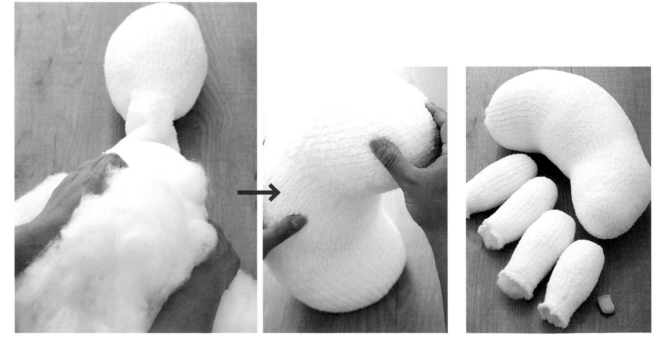

6 Pack a large ball of stuffing densely behind the head to make the body firm. Shape stuffing into a long cylindrical form and smooth between the head and body. Mold a curve where head and body meet.

7 Stuff the legs and pink tongue. Shape each part into a smooth form.

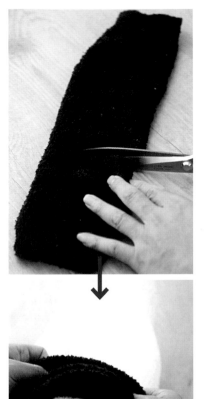

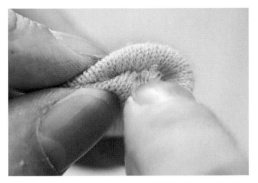

11 Close opening of tongue and hide fringes inside the seam. Stitch tongue to point A with ladder stitches.

9 Use running stitches to close the opening of both layers at the same time. With double stitches, sew through the white and black socks together to securely seal the opening.

8 Cut one of the black socks ⅔ of the way down the leg. Pull the longer piece onto the white body; it should cover half of the body.

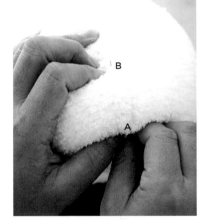

10 At the front of the head, pinch 2 ½ inches (6 cm) of stuffing. With white thread, start at point A and exit at point B. Pull thread tight and repeat three times. Tight stitches will sink into the stuffing forming the line between the nose and mouth.

12 Sew two woolly balls beside each other, and then stitch to point B to make the nose. Position nose directly above tongue.

13 Mold neck to make the head bend down slightly and mark location of the eyes.

14 Sew black buttons on as eyes; be sure they are equal distance from the nose.

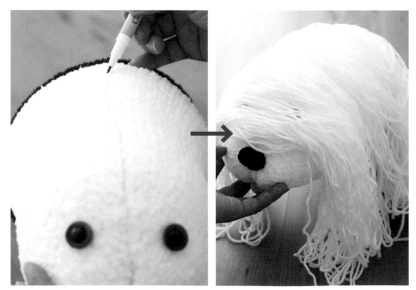

15 Fold two bunches of yarn a few times until they are 1 3/4 inches (50 cm) in length.

16 Mark the center of the head; it should line up with the nose. Spread yarn evenly over center line leaving an equal length on each side.

17 Along the center line, sew yarn onto head in 1⅝ inches (4 cm) wide bunches. Stitch through plenty of stuffing to secure and pull thread tight.

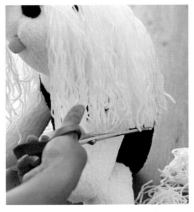

20 Trim yarn on both sides in small increments to find the right length. Do not cut too much at once.

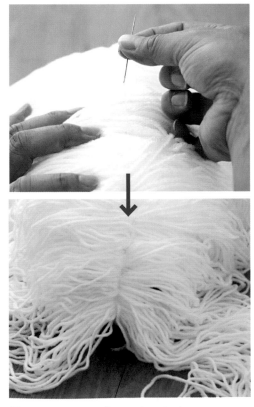

18 Repeat previous step twice. Make sure yarn is stitched firmly onto the head.

19 Use ladder stitches to sew front legs onto the middle of the body and back legs to the bottom. Position back legs at right angles, so the dog sits upright.

21 If yarn is woven together with multiple strands, separate them to make the hair look thicker. This may make the yarn curly, which will give your sheep dog a very cute look.

Dragon

ADVANCED
8

Daniel's Classroom Tips

○ To make the dragon, many pieces need to be stitched together using advanced techniques. To achieve the right look, it is important to stuff each body part densely.

○ You need long and strong needles and strong thread that can go through thick stuffing.

✕ Materials and Tools

1 Black thread for eyes
2 Brown thread for mouth
3 Green thread for body and legs
4 White thread for teeth
5 Large scissors for cutting fabric
6 Tweezers/cuticle scissors for working with small socks, to help turn the fabric inside out, or to help when stuffing
7 Small, pointed scissors for seam ripping
8 Two ¼ inch (0.5 cm) diameter black beads for eyes
9 Erasable marking pen
10 Two needles
11 Three green knee socks for head, body, and tail
12 One pair of dark green toe-socks for legs and fins
13 One white cotton sock for teeth and whites of the eyes
14 One small piece of red felt for inside of mouth
15 Stuffing (not shown in photo)

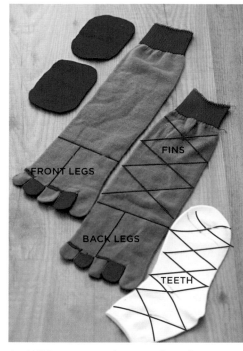

FINS

FRONT LEGS

BACK LEGS

TEETH

1 With your marker, outline the shape of what will become the front legs and back legs, as shown in illustration above. On one of the socks, mark a criss-cross shape for the fins. On the white sock, mark a criss-cross shape for the teeth. Cut the red fleece into two rectangles for the mouth and round corners.

2 Cut out legs, fins, and teeth and turn inside out. Sew seams together on each but leave a small opening for the stuffing. Turn right side out and stuff each piece.

3 Take stuffing, about five times the size of your fist, mold into an oval shape, and stuff to the bottom of a green knee sock to form the head. Pack more stuffing in tightly to form the body. Mold the two pieces of stuffing into a V shape where they connect.

Take your time!

4 For the tail, shape stuffing, about four times the size of your fist, into an oval shape and fill the bottom of the second green knee sock. Add additional ball of stuffing behind the first and mold the connection into a V shape. Leave one third of the sock near the cuff free of stuffing.

5 For the lower jaw, push an oval shape of stuffing to the bottom of the third green knee sock. The lower jaw should be smaller than the head. Cut off the extra sock and close opening.

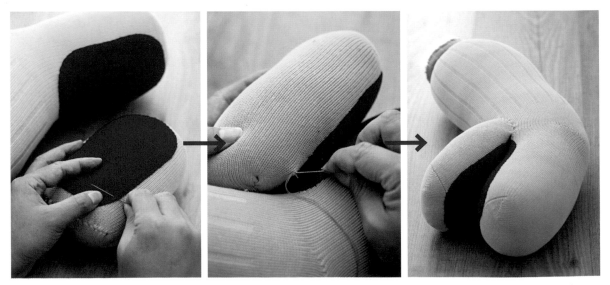

6 Stitch one red felt piece under the head and one on the lower jaw. Use dense ladder stitches to attach the lower jaw to the head at the V shape.

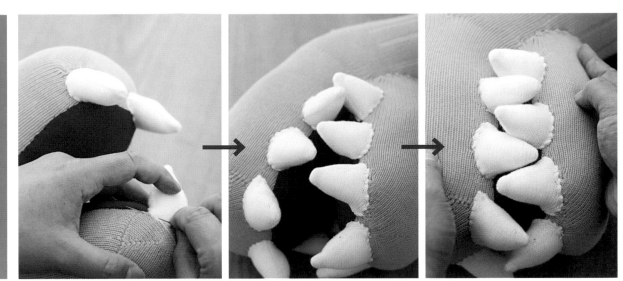

7 Sew the first tooth on in the middle front of the mouth, and then sew the rest on, working toward the back. Position the upper and lower teeth so they interlock.

8 For the whites of the eyes, place a glass on the white sock and trace around the rim.

9 Use running stitches to tighten the opening and make into a ball with a small opening. Stuff the ball and use cross stitches to partially close the opening.

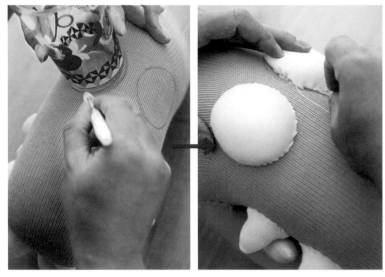

10 Mark the location of the eyes by tracing the rim of a smaller glass. Stitch the whites of the eyes along the circles.

11 Sew the black beads onto the whites of the eyes as the pupils. Pull thread tight so pupils sink into the fabric.

HOW TO MAKE THE TAIL

12 Pull the cuff of the tail onto the body part. You may need someone to hold the parts while you connect them.

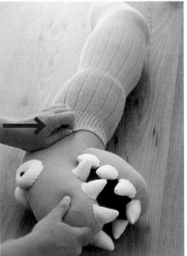

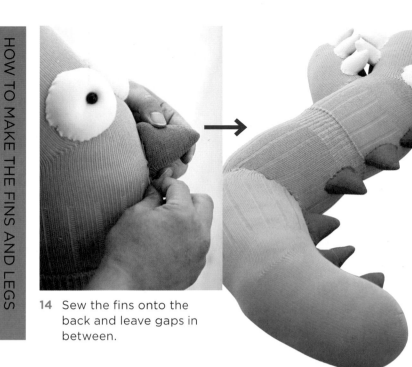

14 Sew the fins onto the back and leave gaps in between.

13 Bend the tail up to form a V shape where it connects to the body. Stitch along the V and pull thread tight to secure the tail in position.

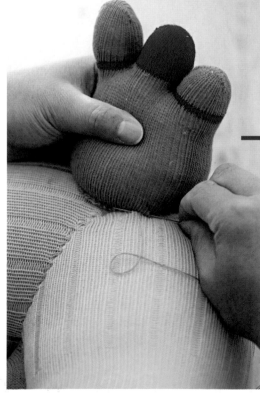

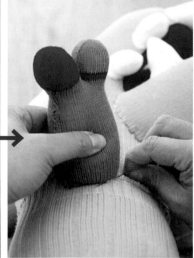

15 Sew front legs to the middle of the body and back legs to where the tail connects to the body. The dragon should be able to sit up and be supported by its legs.